Our American Century

Century of Flight

By the Editors of Time-Life Books, Alexandria, Virginia

Contents

★

Foreword

Over the years as a test pilot I managed to walk away from a few nasty rides, and once had to be carried away, badly burned. But my scariest moment occurred only two stories aboveground, standing stiffly at attention in front of the desk of Colonel Albert G. Boyd, head of the flight test division at Wright Field. I was then a 23-year-old captain, a hot-shot fighter jock who had just completed a tough six-month course to qualify as one of his 25 test pilots that winter in 1946.

I expected the Old Man to lower the boom. As a prank, a couple of us had put pebbles in the hubcaps of his car. "Yeager, you're dead," I told myself. Boyd's bark could peel the skin off a rhino. But this time he just amazed me.

"Yeager," he said, "I'm offering you the most important flight since the Wright brothers." He chose me, his most junior test pilot, to break the sound barrier. He admired my instincts in the cockpit, my ability to keep cool.

Back then, Boyd had authority to decide who would fly the most important Air Corps flight test program of his lifetime without checking his decision with anyone. But if I screwed up, we'd both hang. Only 13 of us were assigned to the mission, living like sand fleas next to a dry lake bed in the Mojave. Ten years later, we were still there, now 125 pilots, testing a new generation of supersonic fighters, interceptors, and bombers. We flew straight wings, sweptwings, and triangular delta wings. Our cockpit electronics were Buck Rogers.

Cracking the sound barrier led to a golden age. Over 55 years, I flew more than 600 different models and types of airplanes, from the 1911 Curtiss Pusher to World War II fighters and most of the supersonic jets. For those of us born to fly, this century was the only time to be alive. We will never see its like again.

Chuck Yeager
B/Gen. USAF Ret.

Old meets new as Wilbur Wright and a passenger soar over horse-drawn carriages in France in 1909. The Wrights enjoyed celebrity status in Europe as they introduced the world to what would prove to be the most momentous invention of the century.

A chorus line high-kicks on the wings of a new Western Airlines luxury passenger airplane in Alhambra, California. With new airlines springing up all over America in the 1930s, promotional gimmicks became a popular way to generate public interest.

Charles Lindbergh poses midflight in April 1936 in his British-built Mohawk. Since his record-breaking flight in 1927, Lindbergh's passion for planes and for flying had never wavered: "I believe the risks I take are justified by the sheer love of the life I lead."

Their smiles as wide as the flight deck, pilots aboard the carrier Lexington celebrate a successful mission in November 1943. Less than two years after Pearl Harbor, well-trained airmen and superior equipment helped break Japan's hold in the Pacific.

A helicopter supplies besieged U.S. marines in
Khe Sanh in 1968. Choppers came to symbolize
America's involvement in Vietnam and were a
welcome sight to GIs in the field—part gunboat,
part hospital, part rescue craft.

"I am very thankful to be the first. . . . This is fun!" exclaimed Ed White as he took America's first spacewalk in 1965. White's happy jaunt had a serious purpose, proving to NASA that astronauts would be able to work in space.

Amid shimmering vapors, a Blackbird spy plane gets the once-over from its ground crew. Tearing through the skies at mach 3, the SR-71 gulped fuel: Its twin engines—as powerful as 45 diesel locomotives—burned 12,000 gallons in 90 minutes.

In hot pursuit, an F-15 pilot zeroes in on a hard-banking F-16 playing the role of the enemy in a training exercise. "After a while," notes one veteran, "you don't waste time thinking about what you have to do. You just do it."

The Pioneering Spirit

★

LIVING THE DREAM TO FLY

He was a dreamer: a crazy birdman to some, an eccentric genius to others, and to an important few, an inspiration. But more than dreams, what Otto Lilienthal *(inset)* had going for him was the spirit of the pioneer—a passion to do what had never been done before, and a determination to never give up in the attempt. In that pioneering spirit, he represented the whole generation of aviation's trailblazers.

As a youth in Prussia in the 1860s, Lilienthal had studied young storks learning to soar and tried to emulate them by strapping on homemade wings and flapping his arms. Convinced that he needed to learn the feel of the air before worrying about propulsion, he created gliders of seven designs, with wings of lightweight willow wands and cotton fabric. Lilienthal would position himself upright in the center of the contraption, then run downhill into the wind, catch an updraft, and soar aloft. Maintaining a precarious balance in the air by shifting his weight or swinging his dangling legs, he managed glides of up to 1,150 feet.

After more than 2,000 flights, tragedy struck. One Sunday morning in 1896, a sudden gust of wind pitched his craft sharply upward, and the glider plummeted 50 feet to earth. The impact broke Lilienthal's spine, and he died the next day. His only regret would undoubtedly have been that he had so much yet to learn.

His eyes set on the horizon, Otto Lilienthal prepares for a glider flight in 1894. This model included a system of wires that were designed to make the wings flap when attached to a small engine.

Crazy for the Skies

Built in 1868 by French sea captain Jean-Marie Le Bris, this needle-nose glider flew unmanned several times. It is shown here mounted on a cart in the first-ever photograph of a heavier-than-air craft.

Over the course of centuries, Otto Lilienthal's own courageous precursors had been trying to defy gravity by donning feathers, homemade wings, or voluminous cloaks and then leaping from towers and high cliffs. But after the French demonstrated in 1783 that they could fly suspended beneath a balloon filled with lighter-than-air gases, pioneers on both sides of the English Channel began serious pursuit of a more ambitious challenge: manned flight in a vehicle heavier than air.

The first researcher to understand the principles of aerodynamics and design a craft to accommodate them was an English nobleman, George Cayley. As early as 1799, Cayley had sketched an idea for a glider with a configuration that would ultimately become standard: fixed wings to provide lift, and a tail with horizontal and vertical surfaces for control. A few years later, he built a small model along these lines that actually flew—the first airplanelike craft ever to do so—and soon he was working on full-scale designs.

Sir George continued building gliders into his old age and prevailing upon others to attempt to fly them. In 1849, he noted that one of his craft, a triplane glider, lifted a 10-year-old boy "off the ground for several yards on descending a hill." Four years later, when Cayley was 80

years old, he talked his coachman into making a trial run. After the glider carried him across a shallow valley—perhaps the first manned flight in a fixed-wing glider—the frightened coachman protested, "Please, Sir George. I wish to give notice. I was hired to drive and not to fly!"

Cayley's ideas inspired his fellow countryman William Samuel Henson, a lace manufacturer with an interest in engineering and a passion for inventing. Henson thought he knew just how machines like Cayley's could be powered. He had seen the first railroad locomotives in England and the steam-powered ships that crossed the Atlantic. In 1843 he patented plans for an "aerial steam carriage"—a kind of locomotive of the air—that was to be propelled by a pair of airscrews. Here, for the first time, was the concept of a propeller to power an aircraft. But after a miniature model failed to achieve flight, Henson abandoned the project, married, and immigrated to America.

A crippling problem with steam propulsion was the weight. Four decades after Henson's failure, a French electrical engineer and inventor, Clément Ader, managed to create a propeller-driven craft that weighed only 653 pounds, including its 20-horsepower steam engine and the pilot. In 1890 Ader got in the cockpit, lumbered forward, rose a scant eight inches off the ground and

In 1875, Thomas Moy tethered his Aerial Steamer —with its twin propellers—to a fountain in a London park and fired up the three-horsepower engine; the Steamer reacted "like a dog on a leash," wrote a historian, racing around wildly and making a few brief, six-inch hops into the air.

traveled through the air for about 165 feet. *Eole,* named for the Greek god of the winds, thus became the first manned aircraft to take off from level ground under its own power. But this still fell short of the breakthrough achievement of sustained and controlled flight.

Ader's obsession with propulsion paled beside that of Hiram Maxim. A versatile Maine-born draftsman, machinist, and engineer, Maxim would eventually rack up more than 250 inventions, including a better mousetrap. He settled in England at age 41 after the British War Of-

fice showed more interest in the machine gun he developed than did the American military. Profits from the gun enabled him to renew a youthful interest in flight, and he set about building a biplane.

Maxim focused almost solely on power. "Without doubt," he wrote in 1892, "the motor is the chief thing to be considered. Scientists have long said, Give us a motor and we will very soon give you a successful flying machine." To this end, he built two lightweight steam engines, each generating 180 horsepower, then designed a

craft big enough to hold them and still get off the ground. It turned out to be a monster *(above)*, weighing some four tons. To test it, he constructed an unusual 1,800-foot track with steel rails for the biplane to run on and a matching set of wooden guardrails to keep it from taking off altogether into uncontrolled flight. During a test run in 1894, just as the plane lifted off, one of the guardrails snapped and the liberated machine "floated in the air," Maxim wrote. A chunk of the guardrail smashed into one of the giant propellers, and Maxim had to abort the flight.

Maxim turned to other interests. He had failed to really fly, but he knew success, for someone, was near. In 1893 he had told a journalist, "Aerial navigation will be an accomplished fact inside of ten years." Two brothers from Ohio would come within weeks of proving him right.

With a wingspan of 107 feet, a length of 200 feet, and two propellers 18 feet in diameter, Hiram Maxim's steam-powered machine rests heavily on its steel track at his estate in England. Outer wooden guardrails restrained the craft from actually taking off.

The Wright brothers—Wilbur (left) and Orville—sit businesslike on their back porch in 1909. They almost always wore suits and ties, even during flight attempts at Kitty Hawk.

The Wright Way

O
n June 2, 1899, a letter arrived at the Smithsonian Institution in Washington, D.C., asking for information on the subject of aviation. "I have some pet theories as to the proper construction of a flying machine," the writer explained, but his intent was the essence of modesty: "I wish to avail myself of all that is already known and then if possible add my mite to help the future worker who will attain final success."

The man at the Smithsonian complied with the request but paid no special heed. Letters from would-be aviators—and just plain cranks— had been streaming in ever since 1896, when the Smithsonian's secretary, the renowned scientist Samuel Pierpont Langley, had successfully flown a steam-powered scale model of an airplane and later received a $50,000 grant from the U.S. Army to build a full-size, man-carrying version.

The writer of the letter was 32-year-old Wilbur Wright. He was the

Soaring above their base camp near Kitty Hawk, North Carolina, one of the Wright brothers gets in some glider practice on October 21, 1903. Bad storms, which had left portions of the beach flooded, briefly delayed attempts with their newer, engine-equipped model, whose historic flight was less than two months away.

"I am an enthusiast, but not a crank."

Wilber Wright, letter to the Smithsonian, 1899

The Wrights' rival in the race to attain manned, powered flight was the astronomer Samuel Pierpont Langley. The white-bearded Langley is shown at bottom right with his pilot, Charles Manly. On October 7, 1903, his Aerodrome was catapulted from atop a houseboat anchored in the Potomac River. The craft, with its tandem wings and 52-horsepower engine, surged forward (inset, right), then nosedived into the river (below). Another failure two months later ended Langley's quest.

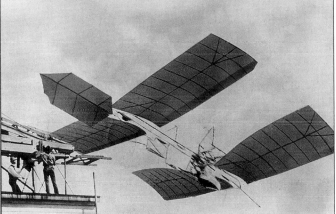

proprietor, along with his 28-year-old brother Orville, of the Wright Cycle Company in Dayton, Ohio. The youngest sons of a single-minded United Brethren bishop and his resourceful wife, who could mend or make almost anything around the house, the Wright brothers were inveterate tinkerers. Besides repairing and custom-building bicycles, they had run a printing business, published newspapers, and built their own press.

The brothers read every book and article recommended by the Smithsonian. They learned that researchers such as Otto Lilienthal had made progress in controlling gliders with elevators, which regulated pitch up and down, and with rudders, which took care of steering to the left or right. But Lilienthal had not mastered a third crucial movement—rolling from side to side—which he had attempted to accomplish by shifting his weight.

Wilbur had a better idea. Untrained academically, he nonetheless possessed the intuitive engineer's ability to isolate the problem, define it precisely, and find the information to solve it. Observing buzzards in flight, he noticed that when a gust of wind knocked them askew, they regained their balance by twisting the dropped wing downward. This maneuver, he surmised, increased the air pressure under that wing and thus lifted it. The brothers then built a biplane kite and tried out this concept, which came to be known as wing warping. With strings, they manipulated opposite wing tips, turning one tip up and the other down, and found they could create roll or restore balance as they pleased.

The Wrights believed that flying, like bicycling, required practice. "If you really wish to learn," said Wilbur, "you must mount a machine and become acquainted with its tricks by actual trial." They built a glider and, in the fall of 1900, tested it on the beach near Kitty Hawk, North Carolina. The winds there were consistently strong enough to lift the glider, the sand eased the impact of landing, and the local postmaster was hospitable; his wife lent her sewing machine for Wilbur to piece

With Wilbur standing by and Orville at the controls, the Wrights' Flyer takes off into the history books as it rises above the end of its wooden launching rail. The Wrights made three more flights that day—December 17, 1903—and then telegrammed their father, who noted their success in his diary (far right).

together the two fabric wings. The brothers camped out, fought black flies and mosquitoes that, Orville later reported, "chewed us clear through our underwear and socks," and took turns flying their creation. When they were finished for that season, the postmaster's wife salvaged enough fabric from the wings for two dresses for her daughters.

They returned the next year with a second glider—built bigger to increase lift. This one proved so difficult to control that it twice went into the kind of midair stall that had killed Lilienthal. Disconsolate, Wilbur predicted, "Nobody will fly for a thousand years!" But they went back to the drawing board. They had based their failed wing design on Lilienthal's old calculations of various lift ratios. Suspecting these tables might be wrong, they built a little wind tunnel and painstakingly tested some 150 different miniature wing shapes in the airstream generated by a fan. The resulting glider was more graceful looking, with longer and narrower wings, and it flew beautifully. In 1902, the brothers made close to 1,000 glides.

They were ready now to add an engine but could not find a suitable one. So, with the help of their bicycle-shop mechanic, Charlie Taylor, they designed and built it themselves: a 140-pound, four-cylinder gasoline engine that produced the 12 horsepower their precise calculations called for. They also had to engineer from scratch the rear-mounted twin propellers that, when connected by bicycle chains to the engine, would push the craft through the air.

Everything seemed to have come together when the Wrights returned to Kitty Hawk in the autumn of 1903. Then came mishaps and delays—and groundless fears that Langley might fly first. The wind blew at gale force, and it turned bitter cold. The propeller shafts were damaged and had to be sent back to Dayton for repair—one of them twice. Wilbur's first attempt to fly the craft covered scarcely 60 feet and ended ignominiously in a crash. But three days later, at 10:35 a.m. on December 17, 1903, his younger brother lay down on the lower wing next to the engine and took off. Orville flew for 12 seconds and landed 120 feet from takeoff. It was history's first manned, powered, and controlled flight. Later that day Wilbur stayed aloft for 59 seconds and a distance of 852 feet. A witness sprinted down the beach shouting, "They have done it! Damned if they ain't flew!"

Rivals Close the Gap

Soon enough, the Wrights had company in the air—the result of a somewhat unlikely collaboration between a relative unknown and one of the most famous names of the day. In 1907, Alexander Graham Bell was 60, white-bearded, and portly; the acknowledged patriarch of American technology, he had been intrigued by the notion of flight for more than 30 years and loved to tinker with unwieldy, weirdly configured kites. Glenn Hammond Curtiss was in his late 20s and gaunt, with a bristly dark mustache and a perpetual frown. A high-school

dropout, he owned a motorcycle factory in Hammondsport, New York, and was obsessed with speed; indeed, he was considered the "fastest man in the world" after riding one of his motorcycles at 136.3 miles per hour.

The pair came together under the auspices of the newly organized Aerial Experiment Association. Bell formed the five-man group, which was financed by his independently wealthy wife, with one purpose in mind: "to get into the air." Curtiss was invited to become one of Bell's Boys, as the group was known, because his powerful, lightweight engines had proved effective in propelling dirigibles. With Bell suggesting ideas and Curtiss supplying technical know-how, the new team built a series of three aircraft in a matter of months.

With their third craft—dubbed June Bug by Bell because of the insects swarming in upstate New York that spring—Curtiss entered a flying competition sponsored by *Scientific American*, which offered a silver trophy for the first public powered flight in the U.S. of more than one kilometer on a straight course. Wilbur Wright already had flown more than 24 miles in a single flight nearly three years before—but secretly, in the seclusion of an Ohio cow pasture. Curtiss invited newsmen, photogra-

---

Glenn Curtiss flies his plane June Bug over a one-kilometer course in 1908 (right), setting the official U.S. record for distance. Above, Curtiss poses at far left with other members of the Aerial Experiment Association, including Alexander Graham Bell at center and Thomas Selfridge at far right.

phers, and leading aviation enthusiasts to Hammondsport. On July 4, 1908, he roared down a racetrack outside town, lifted off, and flew some 2,000 feet beyond the required kilometer. Curtiss won the trophy, nationwide acclaim—and an immediate letter of protest from Orville Wright.

The Wright brothers were upset because the June Bug was equipped with ailerons. These small triangular flaps, mounted on hinges at the ends of both top and bottom wings, controlled the plane's lateral balance much as wing warping did. Bell, who had suggested the concept, denied that he had borrowed the idea from the Wrights. But Wilbur and Orville considered any form of movable wing section to be an extension of wing warping and thus an infringement upon the patent they had been granted in 1906.

They also resented Curtiss because their own accomplishments had received scant recognition. This was partly the fault of the press, but the Wrights themselves were as much to blame. Since their first flight, they

Wilbur Wright assesses conditions at an airfield during his trip to France in 1908 (top). His first flights there in August received wide acclaim in the press (above), and his soft cap—a gift from Orville—became a trademark; soon, "Veelbur Reet" caps were adorning heads all over France.

"I have today seen Wilbur Wright and his great white bird. . . . There is no doubt! Wilbur and Orville Wright have well and truly flown."

Journalist for *Le Figaro,* August 11, 1908

had done their utmost to work in secret lest someone steal the ideas behind their invention, which they hoped to sell. After the U.S. Army repeatedly rejected their overtures, the Wrights went abroad, asking $200,000 for the right to produce their flying machine. Negotiations with the British and French governments broke down largely because the brothers refused to demonstrate their aircraft or even show photographs of it until a contract had been signed.

In 1908, however, the logjam broke. Both a French syndicate and the U.S. Army offered contracts contingent upon successful demonstration flights. The pair went back to Kitty Hawk that spring to brush up their flying skills and modify their craft so that it could carry both the pilot and a passenger sitting up. Then, while Wilbur sailed for France to show off their newest model, Orville put together another craft for the trials in September to nail down the $25,000 army contract.

Orville awed the army brass at Fort Myer, Virginia. He had no difficulty meeting the required specifications, which included flying nonstop for 10 miles at an average speed of 40 mph. He repeatedly exceeded his own endurance records, finally staying aloft for more than 70 minutes. But Orville was concerned by the presence of a man he considered an enemy—army lieutenant Thomas Selfridge, a member of Bell's Aerial Experiment Association. Selfridge was also a member of the official army aeronautics board, and on September 17, he accompanied Orville on a flight. Some 150 feet up, one of the two propellers cracked, setting off a chain reaction that snapped a wire to the rudder. The craft veered out of control and crashed nose first. Selfridge died that evening—history's first airplane fatality. Orville suffered several injuries but

survived to successfully complete the trials 10 months later.

In France, meanwhile, Wilbur at first encountered skepticism. He silenced the critics in a series of breathtaking flights before thousands of spectators, including kings and queens. On one occasion he stayed aloft for nearly two and a half hours, covering 77 miles. He was later joined by Orville, hobbling on two canes but able to fly. The French in particular were intrigued by these eccentrics who did not smoke, drink, gamble, chase women, or fly on Sunday. Treated like royalty wherever they went in France, Italy, and England, the Wrights captivated Europeans with their down-to-earth manner. Invited to make a speech, Wilbur replied, "I know of only one bird, the parrot, that talks, and it doesn't fly very high."

When the Wrights returned to the U.S. in 1909 to

Rescuers work to extricate the injured Orville Wright from the wreckage of his biplane at Fort Myer, Virginia, on September 17, 1908. Wright's passenger, Lieutenant Thomas Selfridge, lay dying nearby among torn canvas and cables—the first person ever killed in an airplane. Mourning the loss, French aircraft builder Gabriel Voisin wrote of "the wings that fly, the wings that kill."

Jubilant spectators raise their hats as pilot Henry Farman nears the finish line of a one-kilometer circular course near Paris; the flight, in January 1908, was officially the world's longest at the time. Farman, the son of a Paris-based London newspaper correspondent, spoke French better than English and often spelled his first name Henri. In the photograph opposite, he poses at left with the plane's builder, Gabriel Voisin.

overdue acclaim—a White House reception and a celebration in their hometown of Dayton—they left behind a Europe awakened to their invention's enormous potential. The Wrights, wrote an English army major, are "in possession of a power which controls the fate of nations."

The French Go Flying. Even before the Wrights' triumphant visit, the Europeans most eager to overtake the American lead in aviation had been the French. Interest there was galvanized in 1903 when a friend of the Wrights', French-born American engineer and flying enthusiast Octave Chanute, lectured in Paris. Chanute described the Wrights' progress with gliders and even provided sketchy details on their wing-warping concept. Fired by the news that the Americans were ahead, Frenchmen experimented with wing warping but settled instead on ailerons.

The first pilot to achieve manned, powered flight after the Wrights was an adopted son of France, Alberto Santos-Dumont. The heir to a prosperous Brazilian coffee planta-

tion, Santos went to Paris to study in 1891, when he was 18, and stayed. He soon became familiar to Parisians from a series of experiments with dirigibles, which he sometimes set down outside his favorite café. In 1906 Santos put together a biplane that appeared so ungainly someone described it as looking like a tailless goose, attached a 50-horsepower engine, and affixed small ailerons. He got off the ground twice—covering 722 feet on the second flight. Skeptical of reports about the Wrights, Santos at first erroneously thought he was the first to achieve heavier-than-air flight.

Other Frenchmen were also at work. Gabriel Voisin, a dashing young former architectural student who liked to brag about his sexual conquests, teamed up with his brother Charles to establish the world's first aircraft factory near Paris (Gabriel had started building gliders for others as early as 1905). One of their first biplanes, modeled roughly after the Wrights' craft, broke in half during takeoff. A subsequent model, which was piloted by Henry Farman, won a prize early in 1908 by

French pilot Louis Blériot heads out over the waters of the English Channel on the morning of July 25, 1909 (above). After completing the historic crossing, he poses beside his monoplane (right) with his wife, who had followed the flight's progress in a boat.

"I saw something like a huge butterfly dart across the sky."

British policeman as Blériot flew overhead, 1909

completing a circular course a kilometer in length *(page 41)*.

Though the Voisins became prominent producers of flying machines, it was a former client of Gabriel's who electrified aviators in 1909. A man of passionate intensity, Louis Blériot had made a fortune manufacturing automobile headlights and impulsively spent it all, along with his wife's dowry, on building and then crashing experimental monoplanes. Blériot wanted to go after a prize of $5,000 offered by the London *Daily Mail* for the first flight across the English Channel, but he was bankrupt and could not afford a new plane. Then his wife happened to save a young boy as he was about to fall off a Paris

apartment-house balcony. The grateful father, a wealthy Haitian planter, agreed to finance Blériot's Channel attempt.

The odds appeared stacked against Blériot when he took off from near the French port of Calais at 4:41 on the morning of July 25, 1909. True, he had successfully adopted the wing-warping idea after seeing Wilbur Wright fly in France the previous year. But his wing had a relatively small surface area and thus marginal lift. His front-mounted 25-horsepower engine—underpowered and crudely made—vibrated noisily, ran hot, and spit oil back into Blériot's face. He had no instruments, not even a compass. Nevertheless, exactly 37 minutes after takeoff,

Blériot landed in an opening amid the white cliffs of Dover —where he was greeted by British customs inspectors.

Blériot's unlikely success dramatized the rapid progress of European efforts. He opened a factory, and the orders came streaming in for the famous monoplane whose single pair of wings would set the pattern for later aircraft.

Back in the United States, Glenn Curtiss and the Wrights formed their own aircraft companies—and engaged in endless legal wrangling. Orville and Wilbur filed lawsuits against Curtiss and several French companies, charging infringement of patents covering control of an aircraft. Instead of enhancing the technology of their old biplane design, they poured all their creative energies into waging these patent wars. "We made the art of flying possible," declared Wilbur, "and all the people in it have us to thank."

By the time the courts upheld their patents in 1914, Orville was preparing to sell their company, and Wilbur was dead. Wilbur died in 1912 at the age of 45, the victim of typhoid fever that racked a body already weakened by the stress of their legal battles. Meanwhile, Blériot, Voisin, and the other French builders were churning out design after design, their work subsidized by a government that was girding for the possibility of war.

Showing Off

Less than a month after Louis Blériot's historic crossing of the English Channel in July 1909, a galaxy of the world's top aviators gathered at the old French cathedral town of Reims. The occasion was the first international air meet, and it marked a rite of passage for this nascent practice of flying heavier-than-air machines. Lured by the substantial prize money put up by the region's champagne makers, more than a score of pilots competed. Virtually every aviation pioneer was there except Orville and Wilbur Wright, who were represented by six of their French-owned biplanes. The planes "wheeled, circled, swooped, vanished and returned with such swiftness and grace," marveled the London Daily Mail, that they created "a spectacle such as has never before been witnessed."

Every record for speed and endurance previously established was shattered during the single week of flying at Reims. French planes and pilots dominated the competition. Henry Farman, piloting a new biplane of his own design, captured the endurance prize with a flight of more than three hours that exceeded 100 miles. The only American airman present, Glenn Curtiss, came equipped with a new eight-cylinder, 50-horsepower engine. He edged out Louis Blériot for fastest average speed by racing around the rectangular 10-kilometer course at an average of 48 mph.

Reims generated so much excitement that airshows proliferated all over Europe and the United States. Only the onset of World War I brought a temporary end to the practice.

Eugène Lefebvre banks his Wright biplane around a pylon as he races at Reims (top); two weeks later, the bold Frenchman crashed and died. The prospect of danger only added to the allure of the airshows depicted in these posters.

Battles for the
High Ground

★

WORLD WAR I IN THE AIR

They were witnesses to the turning of an age. Still unaccustomed to the sputtering roar of an airplane engine overhead, the French cavalrymen at left—on their way to World War I's brutal front lines—couldn't have known how profoundly their world would be changed by flying machines. Even though aircraft would have relatively minor impact on the horrific fighting in the trenches and the war's final outcome, the airplane's potential in combat—as reconnaissance craft, bomber, and fighter—was already proving itself.

World War I had complex roots in European politics, and America stayed out of the fray, officially, until 1917. But the lure of flying with an idealistic purpose drew some Americans to the fight earlier. In the spring of 1916, American volunteers formed a squadron called the Lafayette Escadrille, after the French general who had served so nobly in the American Revolutionary War. More than 200 statesiders flew in this and other French units, sharing with their Allied brethren a respect for their enemy counterparts that was returned in full measure. In the midst of the mass carnage—where individuality had lost its meaning—these men stood out. Even as they set the stage for warfare's future, these champions of the high ground recalled its chivalric past. They were thus, in a sense, both the first and the last of their kind.

Carrying drawn sabers and rifles, French cavalrymen watch an Allied biplane heading to the front. Stars on the commemorative flag above honor the 65 Americans who died flying with the Lafayette Escadrille squadron.

A Sopwith biplane takes off from the British carrier HMS Pegasus, which also launched seaplanes by lowering them into the water. Ship-based planes flew reconnaissance and bombing missions at sea and over land.

Finding a Role

The days were dark for the Allies in August 1914. French forces had suffered half a million casualties in that first month of the war alone, and Germany already occupied a quarter of the country. Now, at the end of August, Paris itself was on the brink of falling; German troops were only 25 miles away, and from their front lines they could see the tip of the Eiffel Tower. German planes regularly flew over the city, occasionally dropping leaflets that read, "The German Army is at the gates of Paris. There is nothing for you to do but surrender."

The dire situation was at least in part a result of not knowing what the enemy was up to; both the French and the recently arrived British Expeditionary Force (BEF) had blindly stumbled into catastrophic battles at the war's outset. Neither side had used airplanes effectively for reconnaissance, mostly because observers weren't trained to recognize features from the air and had missed crucial details. Now, in

Paris, the French military governor General Joseph-Simon Gallieni was desperate for information. For several days, both British and French fliers had been scouting, but their reports were a jumble, and at one point Gallieni complained with exasperation that they "amounted to almost nothing!"

Just then, a French pilot brought in a new report, and a British flier confirmed it: The Germans were making a move to the east that left them temporarily vulnerable. Gallieni, suddenly calm, said, "We will fall on the back of their neck."

The Allies struck with everything they could muster, opening a serious gap in the German line and threatening to cut off their westernmost

---

Both sides used tethered balloons (above) as observation posts along the front lines. The hydrogen-filled balloons became tempting targets for aircraft.

"The war comes through the air . . . dripping death."

H. G. Wells

With a wingspan of 140 feet, the German Zeppelin Staaken bomber (below) was the largest of the war. It took a crew of seven to fly the unwieldy craft, including a second pilot to help handle the controls. Bombing raids by both sides, which often killed civilians, delivered terror out of all proportion to their destructive impact and gave a glimpse of warfare's future.

wing. The Germans managed to close ranks, but their offensive had been stopped. Paris had been saved.

The airplane—still just 10 years old—had proved its value, and its mission was clear. Soon, both sides were routinely using airplanes to scout enemy positions, and cameras helped solve some of the identification problems by allowing observers to analyze what they had seen back at base. Radio transmitters carried aloft enabled airborne observers to direct their own force's artillery fire—a task that was also supported by fleets of tethered observation balloons *(page 49)* stationed just behind the front lines.

Initially, the notion of using airplanes as an offensive weapon was barely even considered. Some reconnaissance pilots had taken grenades, hand-held bombs, and even steel darts up with them to harass the enemy below, but they had been largely ineffective. A few military planners saw the potential, though, and before long planes were being converted to carry bombs.

The first true bombing raid took place on October 8, when two British planes took off for German territory. One was a new model, a Sopwith Tabloid, which had bombs mounted in racks hanging from the fuselage.

When he reached his target, a dirigible hangar in Düsseldorf, the pilot released his load, which hit squarely on the mark, sending up a tower of flaming hydrogen as the dirigible inside exploded.

War always breeds an escalating response, so designers on both sides set about building bigger planes that could carry more explosives. By the war's last year, mammoth aircraft toting bombs weighing up to 2,000 pounds were aloft. But by that time, everyone's focus was on a different role for the airplane, one that had evolved as pilots became more skilled and the planes they flew more agile.

It had become clear that, in the hands of an expert pilot, the ideal thing for a plane to do was to shoot down another plane. At first, the goal was to intercept reconnaissance aircraft or bombers and bring them down. Then each side began sending up fighters to take on the interceptors. The best planes and the best pilots were now tangling directly with each other, often within sight of soldiers in the trenches. The drama was undeniable. And in a war starved for heroes, it was little surprise that this aerial jousting —dogfighting, they called it—soon became an end in itself.

Strategic Genius

He often rubbed superiors the wrong way and could be prideful to a fault. But U.S. colonel Billy Mitchell (above) had as clear a vision as anyone of the strategic role airplanes could and should play in war. It served him both well and ill.

Inspired by meeting Orville Wright before the war, Mitchell joined the army's newly formed Aviation Section and rose through the ranks. In Europe, he saw right away that aerial forces ought to be deployed in coordinated actions with the army, strafing and bombing at the front but also making runs behind the lines to hit air bases and supply centers. On September 12, 1918, he enacted just such a plan, orchestrating an onslaught of some 1,500 aircraft as artillery and infantry struck below. The strategy led to a resounding victory.

After the war he was so outspoken in promoting air power that the army court-martialed him in 1925 for criticizing policy. He died in 1936, but his ideas took hold—and the next war proved just how right he had been.

Knights of the Air

A steady drone accompanied the silence around the open grave as half a dozen biplanes circled slowly overhead. The gathered mourners— including Billy Mitchell, commander of America's air forces—had built up a pyramid of flowers beside the casket at the graveside, and now they stood with hats in hands. Twice the planes flew over in formation. Then as pallbearers lowered the coffin into the ground, the planes made one more pass in single file. Led by Eddie Rickenbacker, America's rising star, Flight No. 1 of the 94th Aero Squadron came in at 50 feet, their engines cut. As they passed over, each pilot dropped a cascade of flowers on the grave. Raoul Lufbery, their commander, America's Ace of Aces, had been laid to rest.

It wasn't the first and it wouldn't be the last time that fliers would pay tribute to a fallen comrade. Although their losses were small in raw numbers compared with the awful toll in the trenches, airmen on both sides faced nightmare odds. The average life expectancy for pilots and the observers who often accompanied them was about three to six weeks for those just arriving at the front; over the course of the war, France lost a staggering 77 percent of its pilots. For one thing, the planes themselves could be unreliable, and in the heat of combat, pilots often pushed them past their limits. The French Nieuport, for example, was notorious for losing the canvas from its wings in a steep dive. And because they were so flimsy, planes were relatively easy to shoot down; one well-aimed burst of machine-gun fire from a pursuer could cripple the engine, smash the tail or tear off a wing, or worst of all, ignite the fuel tank.

Death could be grisly, and it was particularly so for Lufbery. On the day he died, he had rushed to join a dogfight in a borrowed plane. After engaging the enemy once, he circled away and seemed to be trying to clear a jam in his gun. He had turned to come in again when suddenly his plane burst into flames, apparently struck in the fuel tank by a flam-

---

American ace Raoul Lufbery (left), who led the Lafayette Escadrille with 17 kills, became commander of America's most famous unit, the 94th Aero Squadron. Finally able to fly for their own country after serving in French and British squadrons, Lufbery and other American pilots eagerly donned their U.S. wings (inset, above).

Rules to Fly By

Oswald Boelcke (above), one of Germany's early flying heroes, was a master tactician. His rules for fighter pilots became the official doctrine of the German Air Service.

1. Try to secure advantages before attacking. If possible keep the sun behind you.

2. Always carry through an attack when you have started.

3. Fire only at close range and only when your opponent is properly in your sights.

4. Always keep your eye on your opponent, and never let yourself be deceived by ruses.

5. In any form of attack it is essential to assail your opponent from behind.

6. If your opponent dives on you, do not try to evade his onslaught, but fly to meet it.

7. When over the enemy's lines, never forget your own line of retreat.

8. Attack on principle in groups of four or six. When the fight breaks up into a series of single combats, take care that several do not go for one opponent.

ing bullet. As members of his squadron watched in horror, Lufbery climbed out of the cockpit as the fire engulfed it and—still several hundred feet up—jumped. His burned body was found impaled on a picket fence at the edge of a garden.

But still men begged to get a chance to fight aloft. It was certainly better than slogging through muddy, gory battlefields, and there were honors galore for success. The top fliers rubbed elbows with royalty, were showered with gifts and medals, and often received cash bounties for their kills. Soon the tradition emerged of designating those who had brought down five or more of the enemy as aces; the Germans called pilots with 10 victories Top Guns. Given the chance at such immortality, most pilots who bothered to think about it at all considered the risks well worth it. Many of them, though, cared only about the action itself, relishing the thrills and the opportunity to prove themselves. It was an age-old motivation. Just like the knights of medieval times with whom they were often compared, World War I's dogfighting pilots sought more than anything else the chivalric glory of confronting a foe, man to man, on the "field" of battle.

The Jousting Begins. Dogfighting was a rather haphazard affair at first. Concentrating on reconnaissance, the air services on both sides discouraged engagements with the enemy. Pilots had little to fight with anyway. Some carried their pistols with them, and occasionally the observer in a two-seater might bring along a rifle to take wild shots at enemy fliers. Although it was never confirmed, one French airman claimed that a German pilot had even thrown a brick at him.

By early 1915, though, the Allies were beginning to mount machine guns either at the back of the observer's rear cockpit or on top of a biplane's upper wing, where bullets would be able to clear the spinning propeller. The experiments met with little success. Guns jammed all the time, and the earliest ones carried as few as 50 rounds anyway, emptying in one or two short bursts. But the biggest problem was aiming. Neither rear-mounted guns nor those on the top wing could be effectively brought to bear as pilots dodged and weaved through the skies.

Then, in April 1915, the French introduced a revolutionary innovation. Plane builder Raymond Saulnier had earlier invented a mechanism that was supposed to enable a machine gun to fire cleanly between a propeller's revolving blades. But the device's timing was imperfect, and bullets occasionally slammed into and destroyed the wooden blades. So Saulnier came

Shown here in reconstruction, the Fokker Eindecker revolutionized dogfighting with a machine gun synchronized to fire through the propeller.

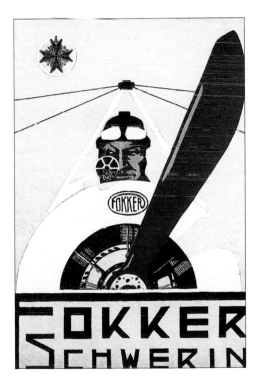

Dutch aircraft designer Anthony Fokker (above, left) stands beside ace Hermann Göring, who would head Hitler's Luftwaffe in World War II. Göring wears Germany's top military medal, the Blue Max, which also appears in the menacing Fokker advertisement at left.

In one of the war's rarest photographs, an Allied two-seater trails smoke as it plummets; the victorious German biplane flies by above. German fighters dominated the war's middle years, only succumbing to the Allies' eventual superior numbers.

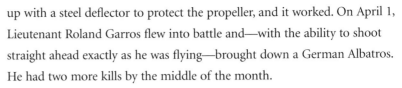

up with a steel deflector to protect the propeller, and it worked. On April 1, Lieutenant Roland Garros flew into battle and—with the ability to shoot straight ahead exactly as he was flying—brought down a German Albatros. He had two more kills by the middle of the month.

The Germans were mystified—until a chance shot from the ground severed the fuel line in Garros's plane on April 18; he glided to a landing in enemy territory, and both he and his plane were captured. The German air command immediately set about copying the innovation—and in the process came up with something even better.

The task had been assigned to entrepreneur and aircraft designer Anthony Fokker, a Dutchman who had immigrated to Germany before the war. Within several days, he and his design team had fashioned a synchronizing mechanism that was foolproof. Mounting it on a superb new airplane, Fokker demonstrated the device himself, then took some of Germany's best pilots up with him to show them how it worked. Among them was a 23-year-old flier named Oswald Boelcke, who had already earned the Iron Cross for flying more than 40 reconnaissance missions.

Boelcke took to the new plane and its synchronized gun right away. "I have attained my ideal with this single-seater," he wrote to his parents. "Now I can be pilot, observer and fighter all in one." Soon he was racking up victories as never before and pushing Germany to preeminence in the air war, a position it maintained even for a while after the Allies had perfected their own firing mechanisms. By the time he was himself downed—his wing having been clipped by the undercarriage of a com-

British artillerymen rush to their antiaircraft guns near Armentières, France, in 1916. The guns could loft 13-pound shells as high as 19,000 feet. Antiaircraft fire terrified pilots on both sides but was largely ineffective at bringing planes down.

"The decisive factor in victory is simple personal courage."

Manfred von Richthofen, 1918

Richthofen's Fokker triplane

Charismatic and gallant, Baron Manfred von Richthofen was the war's top ace, with 80 confirmed kills. After felling his last plane, whose pilot was only slightly injured, Richthofen flew in low and waved to his foe, acknowledging a good fight.

Richthofen's squadron is shown opposite in a typical setting in France: planes lined up beside a flat stretch of field near a town, with tent hangars behind them. Squadrons had to be ready to move quickly to new locations as the lines of battle shifted.

rade's plane—he had 40 kills, the most of anyone at the time, and had literally written the book on dogfight tactics *(page 54)*.

Aces High. Mentors are often surpassed by their protégés, and such was the case with Boelcke. Manfred von Richthofen, a baron by birth, had begun the war in the cavalry but transferred to the air service early on. After a short stint as an observer, he met Boelcke, who encouraged him to apply for pilot training. Initially, it seemed like the wrong move: Richthofen crash-landed on his first solo flight and failed his first pilot's exam. But before long he was matching kills with Boelcke and climbing through the ranks of Germany's airborne elite.

Richthofen had everything it took to be the quintessential knight of the air: the boldness and brashness, unparalleled skill, even the noble lineage, which traced back to Frederick the Great. Taking over Boelcke's role as Germany's top pilot, he scored again and again and again. By April of 1917 he had 45 kills and had for all intents and purposes claimed the skies for Germany. In a move interpreted as both arrogant and foolish,

> "There we were, only a few yards apart, sparring around one another like two prize-fighters in a celestial ring."

Eddie Rickenbacker

Dressed for flight, American aviators in Toul, France, in 1918 mark time in the duty hut while awaiting the signal to take off (above, right). Aviators lived much better than their brethren in the trenches and often sought the nightlife in nearby cities.

Eddie Rickenbacker (opposite) beams his infectious grin in 1916. A former mechanic and racecar driver, Rickenbacker joined the 94th, known as the Hat-in-the-Ring Squadron (emblem, opposite), two years later.

he had painted his Albatros bright red so that it would stand out to friend and foe alike. The squadron he commanded followed suit, and other units did as well, painting their planes in a wide range of garish colors; as a result, the British called them the Flying Circus.

By 1918, the Red Baron had traded his Albatros for a more nimble Fokker triplane *(page 58)*, and the victories continued to pile up. On April 20, he shot down two Sopwith Camels and announced his new total upon landing: "Eighty!" he exclaimed. "That is really a decent number."

It would be his final total. The next day, in a dogfight against two Canadian pilots, a burst of machine-gun fire ripped into his cockpit. Although he managed to land, by the time his triplane rolled to a stop, Richthofen was dead. Having come down in Allied territory, he was buried by his foes, who treated him with full honors. Allied squadron leaders served as his pallbearers, and a wreath sent from British headquarters was inscribed to "our gallant and worthy foe." He was 11 days short of his 26th birthday.

Just six weeks earlier, a new flier had joined America's recently formed 94th Aero Squadron and taken his first flight across German lines, led by his commander, Raoul Lufbery. At 27, Eddie Rickenbacker was old by pilot standards; a former racecar driver serving as chauffeur for the American general staff, he had only made it into the flying corps on Billy Mitchell's special recommendation. He didn't fit in with his more educated, highbrow colleagues. As fellow pilot Reed Chambers put it, "He was big, older, tough as nails. His race track vernacular, his profane vocabu-

"Most of the pilots he killed never knew what hit them. Out of the sun, a quick burst and gone. That was Rickenbacker."

Fellow pilot Reed Chambers

Insignia of the 94th Squadron

lary, didn't set right with the cream of American colleges."

But what did set right with them, and with his superiors, was Rickenbacker's astounding ability in the air. Like Richthofen, he seemed to have a natural talent for the aerial hunt and a killer instinct that shone like fire from his eyes. His very first victory was a case in point. After a series of maneuvers he had managed to get on the tail of a German Pfalz. As he described it later, "At 150 yards I pressed my triggers. The tracer bullets cut a streak of living fire into the rear of the Pfalz tail. Raising the nose of my aeroplane slightly the fiery streak lifted itself like the stream of water pouring from a garden hose. Gradually it settled into the pilot's seat." Soon thereafter, the plane plummeted to the ground. Rickenbacker had been quick to learn that killing the pilot was as good a way as any to bring a plane down.

Rickenbacker relished his victories and kept careful track. To be counted, a kill had to be confirmed, and it was not unusual for Rickenbacker to jump on a motorcycle after landing and race to the front, hoping to find witnesses who had seen the action overhead. By October 1918 he had supplanted Lufbery as the Americans' top ace and had also taken over the 94th as its captain. The war was all but won at this point, but Rickenbacker and his fellow fliers kept up the fight. Less than two weeks before war's end, he recorded his 26th and last kill, the highest total for an American.

After the war, Rickenbacker wrote eloquently of his own exploits and penned moving tributes to his dead comrades. He was particularly struck by the loss of Frank Luke, who had disappeared on a mission behind enemy lines and never been accounted for. It was perhaps as good an end as any ace could hope for. As Rickenbacker put it, "Frank Luke was swallowed by the skies."

Frank Luke lands his Nieuport after a mission to destroy observation balloons; members of the ground crew help stop the plane by grabbing struts. Luke never returned after his last mission and was presumed shot down behind enemy lines.

The
Golden Age

★

The years after World War I have been called flight's golden age, and with good reason. Aircraft designers were dreaming up faster, more powerful planes almost weekly, and there were pilots aplenty ready to push these remarkable new machines to their limits as soon as they were built. Some fliers slaked their thirst for excitement in air races, vying for lavish cash prizes and glittering trophies. Others sought the immortality of being first—first to cross an ocean or circle the globe or break a speed record. Such ventures also brought tangible rewards, but the ultimate payoff was even bigger. Indeed, from this generation of courageous men and women would emerge a handful of the greatest names in the history of American aviation.

Occasionally, flair could seem to outweigh accomplishment. The flamboyant Roscoe Turner, for example, sought publicity by wearing a powder blue tunic, gleaming boots, a polished gold-and-red racing helmet—and flying with a lion cub as copilot *(right)*. But despite the showmanship, Turner was no lightweight. Holder of the transcontinental speed record over the likes of Lindbergh, he overcame a string of misfortunes that included several crashes to win the coveted Thompson Trophy for one of the year's biggest air contests—a closed-circuit race for landplanes—an unprecedented three times. No one else won more than once.

Roscoe Turner and his lion cub copilot Gilmore logged some 30,000 air miles together, flying races all over North America. Gilmore retired to an animal park, where Turner sent monthly checks for his meat supply.

Daring Doolittle

L ife was rough in the gold rush days in Nome, Alaska, and it was especially so for little Jimmy Doolittle, whose carpenter father had moved the family north in hopes of striking it rich. The boy's angelic face, long golden curls, and small stature made him a tempting target for bullies, but they typically got the worst of any encounters. So it would be throughout Doolittle's life: Challenges almost always fell victim to his fierce determination.

Ever eager for action, Doolittle signed up for aviator training when he joined the army in 1917. Ironically, he was such a good pilot that he never saw combat duty, being kept stateside to train others. After the war, he was picked to fly an experimental Curtiss racer in the 1925 international seaplane race, competing for the Schneider Trophy. Despite having little experience flying seaplanes, he won the trophy, much to the annoyance of the navy. The Curtiss Company later employed Doolittle as a demonstration pilot. On one occasion in Chile, where he was hoping to win a large order of fighter planes, he fell two stories from a balcony after clowning around. Despite having casts on both broken ankles, Doolittle flew the demonstration the next day and beat a German competitor out of the contract.

The powerful but wildly unstable Gee Bee won the speed contest at the National Air Races in 1932.

Doolittle earned one of the first doctorates in aeronautics from MIT, and in 1929 he put his knowledge to the proof, making the first completely "blind" flight: taking off, flying a prescribed course, and landing on instruments alone, with a lightproof hood covering the open cockpit.

Leaving the army for Shell Petroleum in 1930, Doolittle joined the national racing circuit, promoting Shell aviation fuels and winning race after race. He somehow managed to survive flying the fast but notoriously dangerous *Gee Bee (above, left),* a plane that claimed the lives of five fellow pilots and ultimately led him to quit racing.

Doolittle returned to the army in World War II and finally got his chance at combat, in truly spectacular fashion. Indeed, he would be best remembered for flying the gutsiest and most inspiring air mission of the war: the 1942 bombing of Japan from carrier-launched B-25s *(page 111).* No one who had known little Jimmy at the beginning would have been surprised.

Doolittle's Records

First to fly across U.S. in less than 24 hours

First to fly completely on instruments

Seaplane speed record (246 mph), 1925

Landplane speed record (296 mph), 1932

Jimmy Doolittle beams in the cockpit of a plane called the Super Solution, having just won the first-ever cross-country race in 1931.

The Lone Eagle

"My back is stiff; . . . my face burns. . . . All I want . . . is to throw myself down flat . . . and sleep."

Charles Lindbergh after 17 hours of transatlantic flying

The huge fuel tank of the Spirit of St. Louis blocked Lindbergh's forward vision; he used a periscope, side windows, and a compass to keep on course.

When Lindbergh landed in Paris, headlines blared the news back home (above). "His daring dazzles the world," said the London Sunday Express.

He was 25 years old but looked 18, and no one outside St. Louis, where he flew an unprofitable airmail route, had even heard of him. Nevertheless, Charles Augustus Lindbergh aimed to be the first to fly nonstop between New York and Paris, and he intended to do it alone. If he succeeded he would win a $25,000 prize—and would pave the way for transatlantic air travel.

Lindbergh wasn't the only one trying for the prize in 1927. Several of the biggest names in aviation were preparing for the contest, with powerful, multiengine planes built by leading aircraft manufacturers. When he showed up in New York in a single-engine plane built by some tiny outfit in San Diego, newspaper editors dubbed him the flying fool. By this time, four attempters had died, three had suffered injuries, and two were missing. What made this young fellow think he could succeed where others, better known and better financed, had failed?

Lindbergh's plan was to simplify. "A plane that's got to break the world's record for nonstop flying should be stripped of every ounce of weight," he noted, and that included an extra man, even though it would mean staying awake for at least 36 hours straight. To eliminate more weight, he sacrificed radio, sextant, lights, fuel gauges, and parachute. When he took off from New York on a rainy morning in May, his stripped-down *Spirit of St. Louis* was so loaded with fuel that it cleared the telephone lines at the end of the field by a mere 20 feet. Most New Yorkers thought they would never see him again. Lloyd's of London refused to quote odds on his chances, because "the risk is too great."

Two nights later, when the exhausted American in the plane with no lights landed in Paris, the world erupted with joy. The president of the French Army Commission of the Chamber of Deputies declared, "It is not only two continents which you have united, but the hearts of all men everywhere in admiration for that simple courage of a man who does great things."

Although Lindbergh made his historic trip alone, he characteristically referred to himself and his plane (right) as "we." No one else ever flew the Spirit of St. Louis.

Up, Up, and Around

An oil-rigging accident cost Wiley Post his left eye, but it didn't deter him from becoming a pilot: He used the insurance payment to buy his first airplane. To make up for lost depth perception, he trained himself to judge distances from other clues and soon had his pilot certificate.

The plane with which Post would forever be associated, a speedy Lockheed Vega named the *Winnie Mae (below, left),* brought him his first taste of fame in 1930, when he won a nonstop race from Los Angeles to Chicago. Post next set his sights on beating the round-the-world record, held at the time by the dirigible *Graf Zeppelin*. With the blessing of his oil developer employer, who owned the *Winnie Mae,* he hired Australian navigator Harold Gatty and planned out the 1931 trip, arranging for spare parts and fuel to be stored along the route, asking permission to fly over other countries, studying weather maps for remote regions, and modifying the *Winnie Mae* with extra fuel tanks and an overhead hatch for sighting stars. Post learned to stay awake for long periods and relied on instruments pioneered by Jimmy Doolittle to get through fog and bad weather. Despite having sunk into mud in Siberia and having wrecked the propeller in Nome, Post and Gatty circled the globe in eight days, 15 hours, and 51 minutes, beating the *Zeppelin's* record by 13 days.

Winnie the Workhorse. *Wiley Post flew the Winnie Mae (above) for his employer, F. C. Hall, a wealthy Oklahoma oilman who wanted a speedy plane and a pilot to help him scout out potential drilling sites. He didn't mind when Post entered the plane—a Lockheed Vega—in air races and flew it around the world in his spare time. The craft's design was revolutionary: Other planes had flat sides along the fuselage, but the Vega's sides were fashioned from rounded plywood half-shells glued together to produce a smooth, strong, and streamlined shape. Although the Winnie Mae (named for Hall's daughter) could accommodate four passengers, Post removed the seats and replaced them with giant fuel tanks for his round-the-world flights.*

Post, who had since bought the *Winnie Mae* for himself, made the same trip solo in 1933, using an automatic pilot and keeping himself awake by holding a wrench tied to one of his fingers: When his grip relaxed, the wrench would jerk him into consciousness. He broke his own record by 21 hours, becoming the first person to fly around the world twice, and the first to do it alone.

But Post's greatest contribution to aviation was more about height than distance. Convinced that the future of air travel depended on flying at high altitudes where the jet stream could increase speed, Post found a way to get there. He knew he could not make the plywood *Winnie Mae* airtight—a necessity for survival in the thin upper atmosphere—so instead he invented a pressurized pilot's suit *(right)* and flew the *Winnie Mae* to nearly 40,000 feet in 1934. A year later he was dead, killed in a seaplane crash along with his passenger, humorist Will Rogers.

In the first successful high-altitude pressure suit, Wiley Post spent more time in the stratosphere than anyone else in the 1930s.

Fallen Star

Amelia Earhart lived long enough to accomplish many of her goals: She crossed the Atlantic solo in May 1932, the first woman to do so; she was the first woman to fly solo across the United States, in July 1932, and the first person to fly from Hawaii to California, in January 1935; and she set a speed record for flying from Burbank, California, to Mexico City in April 1935. But another target loomed.

Although Wiley Post had already circumnavigated the globe, he had flown in the northern latitudes, and no one yet had circled the earth at its widest point, near the equator. Earhart confided to a few friends, "I have a feeling that there is just about one more good flight left in my system, and I hope this trip is it."

The dangers of flying such a tremendous distance, and over so much water, had discouraged others from attempting the equatorial record. But her Lockheed Electra *(left)* was well equipped for the challenge, and she was taking along Fred Noonan, Pan Am's principal navigator.

As she wrote to her husband, George Putnam, before an earlier dangerous flight, "Please know I am quite aware of the hazards. I want to do it because I want to do it. Women must try to do things as men have tried. When they fail, their failure must be . . . a challenge to others."

Earhart took her role model status seriously. She had begun teaching classes part time at Purdue University, where she hoped to encourage other mechanically minded girls to pursue their dreams as she had. One of her ambitions was to set up a machine shop "where girls may tinker to their heart's content with motors, lathes, jigsaws, gadgets . . . where they may sprawl on their back, peering up into the innards of engines . . . where they can make things and have the fun of finding out how things are made, why engines perk, clocks tick, radios yowl."

On July 2, 1937, Earhart and Noonan began the last leg of their round-the-world flight, heading from New Guinea to tiny Howland Island, 2,500 miles away. Before and after they were due, Earhart sent several radio messages indicating they couldn't find Howland. Then silence. The U.S. Navy swept the area for 16 days with planes and ships, but they found no trace of plane or crew.

Globetrotting Electra. *Towering over Earhart and her Cord Cabriolet convertible, the twin-engine Lockheed Electra (above) took the travel-loving aviator places her automobile couldn't: Hawaii, Venezuela, Brazil, Senegal, Sudan, India, Burma, Thailand, and New Guinea. Until she and her navigator were lost in the South Pacific, the all-metal Electra had carried them safely some 22,000 miles around the world. Purdue University had purchased the plane for Earhart as a "flying laboratory" in connection with the classes she taught there, testing such things as the effect of altitude on metabolism. But Earhart was also free to use the plane as she chose and adapt it accordingly. Some of the changes made for her round-the-world attempt were never blueprinted and remain as mysterious as the plane's final resting place.*

"When I was a little girl in Kansas," Earhart wrote, "the adventures of travel fascinated me. . . . As the girl grew older, the inclination did not mend."

> "I intend to be . . . the finest film producer in Hollywood, the greatest pilot in the world, and the richest man in the world. But not in that order."
>
> Howard Hughes, age 19

The Millionaire Aviator

Howard Hughes approached aviation the same way he did other pursuits: with a serious, scientific quest for perfection and a generous amount of cash. Sole heir of Texas tycoon Howard Hughes Sr., who had invented a drill bit used on almost all oil-drilling operations in the world, young Howard grew up pampered, sheltered, shy, and lonely, and at age 18 inherited $17 million when his father died. He promptly bought out his relatives' shares of the Hughes Tool Company and took off for Hollywood.

To succeed at golf—an early passion—he joined all three country clubs in Los Angeles, hired the best golf pros, and had his practice sessions filmed at ground level and from a blimp, in slow motion and in Technicolor. To succeed at moviemaking, he spent $4.2 million of his own money producing, directing, and even stunt-flying in his air war epic, *Hell's Angels*—for which he had collected more than 40 authentic World War I warplanes from the United States, Great Britain, France, and Germany.

And to succeed at aviation, Hughes hired a team headed by the most innovative designer at Caltech, instructing them to build the fastest plane in the world, which they did *(left)*. He later spent three years planning a round-the-world flight, buying and discarding two airplanes before deciding on the Lockheed Lodestar. Hughes installed the most sophisticated radios and navigational equipment available, and set up a chain of radio-equipped ships and ground stations to keep in constant contact with him. Following roughly the same route as Wiley Post had in his solo flight five years earlier, Hughes and his four-man crew cut Post's time in half, made no unscheduled stops, and never strayed more than six miles off course for the entire 14,824-mile flight. A crowd of 25,000, attracted by frequent reports of the flight's progress, greeted their arrival at New York's Bennett Field.

The venture reportedly cost $300,000 but was well worth it for Hughes. The flawless achievement earned him the Collier Trophy in 1938, which cited him for demonstrating "the value of organization and planning in long-range aircraft operation."

The Silver Bullet. *"I want you to build me the fastest airplane in the world," Howard Hughes told his team of scientists, engineers, and mechanics in 1933, and swore them to secrecy. Two years and $120,000 later, the H-1 racer, also known as the Silver Bullet, broke the landplane record with a top speed of 354 miles per hour before smashing into a California beet field. It was later discovered that a gas line that had been plugged with steel wool caused the crash, from which Hughes emerged unharmed. The plane was repaired, and in 1937 Hughes flew it to a new transcontinental record of seven and a half hours. He retired the H-1 shortly thereafter, having flown it a total of only some 40 hours.*

Howard Hughes stands beside the Lockheed Lodestar that carried him around the world in a record-breaking three days, 19 hours, and 17 minutes.

Pilot Lincoln Beachey edges his Curtiss biplane ahead of racecar driver Barney Oldfield's Fiat in 1914—a contest they repeated across the country.

Thrilling the Crowd

In the early years after the Wright brothers' invention, daring exhibition fliers such as Lincoln Beachey *(left)* were eager to prove what airplanes could do. Beachey thrilled onlookers by looping loops, flying upside down, zipping his biplane in and out of ball fields and under telephone lines, and even diving into the mists of Niagara Falls. Some of the techniques he and others developed for their performances later proved useful to military pilots during World War I.

After the war, the U.S. government sold off hundreds of excess airplanes at cheap prices to recently decommissioned fliers, and barnstorming began. Named for the gypsy pilots who skimmed the cow pastures and grazed the barns of rural America looking for passengers who might pay five dollars for a five-minute ride, barnstorming brought flying into everyone's backyard.

Founder Bon MacDougall (above, right) welcomes Reginald Denny into the 13 Black Cats, stunt pilots who charged set fees for their tricks (below).

At the 1935 Minnesota State Fair, pilot Frank "Bowser" Frakes performs his trademark stunt of crashing into a building, a trick that later cost him his life.

Black Cats Stunt Price List

Fixing prices on occasionally fatal stunts, the Black Cats offered a menu of thrills:

Crash plane (fly into trees, houses, etc.)	$1,200
Loop with man standing on wings	450
Plane change	100
Change—motorcycle to plane	150
Fight on wing, one man knocked off	225
Upside-down flying with man on landing gear	150
Head-on collision with automobile	250
Blow up plane in midair, pilot chutes out	1,500

In the sequence above, barnstorming king Ormer Locklear demonstrates some of the tricks that made him famous. He earned as much as $3,000 a day performing aerial feats for grandstand crowds and in Hollywood motion pictures.

Hanging by his knees from the landing gear of a low-flying plane, a barnstormer reaches for a cap in this 1924 stunt.

Highway in the Sky

★

THE BIRTH OF COMMERCIAL AVIATION

There was adventure to be had aloft, but more often than not, what flying was really about was making a buck. Not long after World War I, fledgling airlines in western Europe began transporting passengers in modified bombers. In the United States, carrying the mail proved much more profitable, largely because of government subsidies. A 150-pound passenger flying 1,000 miles would have had to pay a prohibitive fare of $450 for the space to be worth it to the airline. Early passengers even had to agree that airlines could dump them along the route if the company came up with mailbags to take their place.

But still people wanted to and did fly. They endured paralyzing cold and noise so deafening that the pilot communicated with them by scribbling notes. Travelers on Western Air Express *(inset)* had to wear coveralls and a helmet and goggles, strap on a parachute harness, and then sit atop the mail sacks. In 1931 a Fokker Trimotor crashed in a Kansas cow pasture, killing the famed Notre Dame football coach Knute Rockne and six other passengers. Federal inspectors found that the craft had come apart in midair, evidently from rot inside the huge wooden wing. Instead of scuttling commercial aviation, however, the tragedy set the stage for a radical transformation of air travel. It was much needed—and it took.

National Air Transport patrons pay fares for their "mail express" at a runway ticket office (right). The 1928 advertisement above promotes Western Air Express passenger service featuring the Fokker Trimotor.

Better Ways to Go

The plane that cost Knute Rockne his life belonged to an up-and-coming young company, Trans-continental and World Air (TWA). The airline quickly switched to the safer all-metal Ford Trimotor, but it was slow and clumsy, and in 1932 TWA asked manufacturers to come up with a truly modern airliner that could fly faster and farther and be more comfortable. In Santa Monica, California, Donald Douglas, who had founded his own aircraft company 12 years earlier, set his engineers to work right away. Within 10 days they had drawn up plans for a plane that exceeded TWA's specifications.

The 12-seat DC-1—for Douglas Commercial No. 1—offered such innovations as cabin heaters and soundproofing, dual side-by-side controls for pilot and copilot, and an automatic pilot. The wings were so strong they could handle the stress of a steamroller driving over them. Though the DC-1 had only two engines—TWA had specified three—it passed the test insisted on by the airline's technical adviser, Charles Lindbergh: climbing over the highest mountain on their routes with one engine shut down.

By the time the DC-1 was delivered to TWA in 1933 for the bargain price of $125,000, Douglas was ready to build the bigger, better DC-2, which held 14 passengers. Then, at the request of American Airlines, which wanted an overnight sleeper for its transcontinental route, Douglas widened the fuselage to accommodate 14 berths. The daytime version with 21 seats became the plane that revolutionized commercial air travel—the DC-3. Introduced in 1936,

United Air Lines stewardesses show off their 1939 outfits in front of a DC-3—showpiece of aircraft maker Donald Douglas (right). A United poster (top) boasts of DC-3 service between the San Francisco and New York World's Fairs in 1939.

PAN AMERICAN MAKES THE WORLD *SMALLER*

*One of Pan Am's early clippers soars over the
unfinished Golden Gate Bridge on its first
airmail flight to Manila in 1935. The airline
heavily promoted its global reach (inset).*

the DC-3 freed airlines from dependence on airmail contracts. For the first time, they could make money just by hauling passengers. By 1939 three out of every four American air travelers were flying on a DC-3.

Clipper Ships That Flew. To Juan Trippe, the founder of Pan American Airways, naming his big planes clippers was perfectly natural. After all, they were flying boats—equipped with pontoons to land on water—and his well-off family came from an old line of English seafarers. Starting small in 1927, Trippe had launched the first regularly scheduled international service by a U.S. airline, flying the mail and then passengers in a Fokker Trimotor on the 90-mile run between Key West and Havana. His next step was to expand Pan Am into Central and South America.

To handle coastal routes—and more passengers—he commissioned the first of his large, luxurious flying-boat clippers, which had room for 50, then spent millions more on a bigger version that would have the range to fly across the Pacific in a series of hops. In 1936 Trippe began passenger service between San Francisco and Manila. Along the five-day, 8,000-mile route, his China Clippers—so named in anticipation of regular flights to China—refueled and resupplied at bases he had constructed on Midway, Guam, and Wake Island. With the clouds of war already gathering, U.S. Navy officials backed Trippe's efforts as a counter to potential Japanese expansion in the Pacific. But for most people, such exotic locales only symbolized how fast the world was shrinking—because of airplanes.

On a runway in Panama in 1929, Pan Am's founder, Juan Trippe (right), confers with his consultant, Charles Lindbergh. In addition to advising Trippe on technical matters, Lindbergh flew the South American jungles to scout for airfield locations.

Passengers aboard a Pan Am clipper enjoy full meal service with silverware, china, and other dining comforts of a luxury ocean liner. The cabin's walls were lined in walnut.

Fiery End for the Dirigible Dream

The first aircraft to provide passenger service across the Atlantic embodied the dream of the soldier for whom it was named. In 1900, Count (or Graf) Ferdinand von Zeppelin, a former German cavalry officer, had developed the first dirigible, or rigid airship—a steel-framed, lighter-than-air craft driven by propellers and containing cells filled with hydrogen. One of its descendants, the *Graf Zeppelin*, began service between Germany and Brazil in 1931. A marvel of safety and comfort, it made 590 flights, carried more than 13,000 passengers, and clocked over one million air miles.

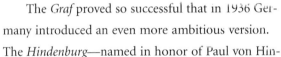

The *Graf* proved so successful that in 1936 Germany introduced an even more ambitious version. The *Hindenburg*—named in honor of Paul von Hindenburg, the former German president—set a standard for luxurious air travel that would never be matched. In addition to 25 double-berth private cabins, it included a 50-foot-long dining room, a lounge with grand piano, a smoking room and bar, and even a writing room. Four 1,100-horsepower diesel engines propelled the craft at a cruising speed of 84 mph. All it lacked was the helium that the designers had specified should fill its gas cells. Because the only supplier, the U.S., refused to export helium, the *Hindenburg* made do with flammable hydrogen.

During 1936, the craft was fully booked with 50 passengers for each of its 20 Atlantic crossings. On May 6, 1937—the first flight of the new season—it completed an uneventful 65-hour voyage and prepared to land at Lakehurst, New Jersey. As it hovered about 75 feet above the ground, a spark—either from static or the natural electrical discharge known as St. Elmo's fire—suddenly ignited leaking hydrogen in the tail section. Flames consumed the enormous craft in just 32 seconds. Somehow, 61 of the 97 persons aboard survived—but not the dream of travel by zeppelin.

Flaming hydrogen erupts from the stern of the stricken Hindenburg, silhouetting ground crewmen on the mooring mast at Lakehurst, New Jersey. The poster above depicts the swastika-adorned craft sailing over Manhattan.

Wings of Victory

★

AIR POWER IN WORLD WAR II

No other instrument of war had ever cast such an immense and ominous shadow. From the German Stuka dive bombers that screeched down over Poland in 1939 as World War II began to the American B-29 Superfortresses that dealt nuclear destruction at its end in 1945, air power played a dominant and frequently decisive role.

Extraordinarily versatile, the airplane exceeded the hopes of its most enthusiastic prewar advocates. It dropped lethal bombs large and small, launched torpedoes, fired machine guns, and, in the hands of Japan's kamikaze suicide pilots, itself became a weapon. Aircraft sank ships, attacked submarines, blew up tanks, terrified infantrymen, shot down other aircraft, destroyed factories, and leveled entire cities. They ferried soldiers and supplies and delivered gliders and paratroopers. They found men lost at sea and evacuated the desperately wounded.

As in World War I, action in the air often led to fame and glory for individual pilots. But fighting aloft was more than ever a group effort, as bombers with 10 man crews teamed in massive squadrons with clusters of fighter escorts swarming all about. The United States was quick to acknowledge the change with the newly instituted Air Medal (*above*), primarily intended to recognize crew members who had completed a set number of combat missions. There was, it was deemed, a certain valor merely in surviving it all.

Escorted by the shadows of its aerial companions, a U.S. B-25 Mitchell bomber flies over North Africa in 1943. Fighters, bombers, and reconnaissance planes played crucial roles in every theater of the war.

The Battle of Britain

Never before had a nation's fate been determined by what was happening in the skies overhead. In June 1940, fresh from victory over France, Germany launched its powerful Luftwaffe against Great Britain. Hitler's aim was to achieve air superiority in preparation for invading the island in September. The Germans counted on strong numerical odds: an armada of nearly 1,800 bombers and fighters against perhaps half that many interceptors of the British Royal Air Force. To lure the RAF into battle, the Luftwaffe struck first at shipping in the English Channel and then, in mid-August, at air bases in southern England.

The British defenders fought back bravely under Air Chief Marshal Hugh Dowding. His Spitfire and Hurricane pilots were astonishingly young—rarely older than 23—but skilled nonetheless. By early September, however, the RAF was reeling under the bombing of its bases. For the first time, the British were losing more planes than they could produce.

Instead of delivering the knockout punch, the Germans changed tactics. On September 7—in retaliation for British raids on Berlin, which had themselves been a response to an unintentional German bombing of London—the Luftwaffe began attacking the British capital. The RAF, their bases now unmolested, swarmed to the attack. On September 15, nearly 300 British fighters filled the skies at once, capping a nine-day period in which the Germans lost 175 planes. Two days later, Hitler postponed his invasion of England indefinitely.

Though the Luftwaffe blitz would continue, the RAF had won the Battle of Britain—and the nation's gratitude and affection. Reflecting on Prime Minister Winston Churchill's habit of calling his airmen Chicks, Dowding noted, "He could have said nothing to make me more proud; every Chick was needed before the end."

At an RAF base in southern England, pilots rush to their fighters on July 25, 1940. During the height of the Battle of Britain, overworked airmen had to "scramble"—take off to meet German attacks—up to eight times a day. Warnings of impending raids came from civilian observers and from radar stations along the coast.

A British Hurricane loses its wing to gunfire from the German fighter that took this picture; Dover's white cliffs are visible at the bottom of the frame.

"Never in the field of human conflict was so much owed by so many to so few."

Winston Churchill, August 20, 1940

Winston Churchill examines the bombed-out House of Commons after an incendiary raid. He vowed to resist German aggression to the very last.

Striking back at the Third Reich, B-17 Flying Fortresses of the U.S. Eighth Air Force drop incendiary bombs on a German factory. These planes belonged to the 303rd Bombardment Group, known as Hell's Angels.

Bombing Around the Clock

Pilot and copilot

Bombardier/nose gunner

Navigator/nose gunner

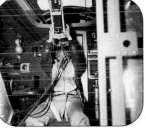
Radio operator/gunner

Two waist gunners

Flight engineer/upper-turret gunner

Ball-turret gunner

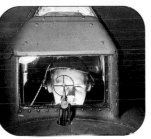
Tail gunner

The 10-man crew of a B-17 bomber, shown in the images above, was a team trained for versatility. Each man was a specialist but was also prepared to perform at least one of the other jobs.

To the recently appointed commanding general of the U.S. Eighth Air Force *(insignia, below),* it was a task nearly as daunting as flying a bomber over enemy territory. On January 20, 1943, at the meeting of Allied leaders in Casablanca, Ira Eaker had to face Prime Minister Winston Churchill and try to change his mind about bombing strategy. In order to destroy factories and other strategic sources of enemy strength, the United States wanted to bomb Germany in the daylight. This strategy already had been attempted unsuccessfully by the RAF—and indeed by the Luftwaffe over Britain. After British bombers had proved to be sitting ducks for German interceptors, the RAF had switched to attacking only at night. Now Churchill wanted Eaker's bombers to join them.

Eaker, who had studied both law and journalism and had a knack for concise argument, presented Churchill with a one-page summary of the case for daylight bombing. Churchill read it aloud. The U.S. B-17 and B-24 bombers were armed with up to a dozen .50-caliber machine guns to defend themselves. They also carried the new Norden bombsight, which promised unprecedented accuracy against factories and other targets from 20,000 feet. But it was a particularly felicitous turn of phrase by the American general that caught Churchill's imagination: "By bombing the devils around the clock, we can prevent the German defenses from getting any rest."

Churchill was still skeptical, but willing to be shown. He agreed to formally endorse a combined, round-the-clock bombing offensive—the Americans by day, the British by night—to prepare for the eventual Allied invasion of western Europe.

A week later, while the British continued their campaign of so-called area bombing—night attacks by armadas of up to 1,000 planes on entire cities—the U.S. made its first strikes into Germany. Until then, all of the fewer than 30 missions flown by Eaker's Eighth Air Force had been directed against targets in France and other occupied coun-

The crew of the Memphis Belle stands by the plane, whose fuselage sports bomb-shaped insignia for the 25 missions they flew and swastikas for the eight enemy planes they shot down. The real-life belle from Memphis was Margaret Polk (inset), sweetheart of the pilot, Captain Robert Morgan (above, fifth from left). Morgan later married another girl—and flew another plane, a B-29 dubbed Dauntless Dottie after his new wife, Dorothy.

tries. Now, aiming at northwestern Germany, his men faced the aerial havoc the British had warned against: heavy barrages of flak—antiaircraft fire—and swarms of speedy Luftwaffe Messerschmitt 109 and Focke-Wulf 190 interceptors. Eaker could put aloft no more than 100 bombers, and he was soon losing more planes and crews than could be immediately replaced. Things were not quite as clockwork as he had hoped.

A Survivor Called Memphis Belle. In early April 1943 the manpower shortage was so grave that Eaker raised the number of missions needed to complete a tour of duty. Going home would now require 30 missions instead of 25. His crews joked that if they did not survive the 25 missions at least they would not have to fly the extra five. But the policy did not apply retroactively, much to the relief of the 10-man crew of the B-17 Flying Fortress known as the *Memphis Belle*.

The plane, christened by the pilot Captain Bob Morgan in honor of his girlfriend, already had flown more than 20 missions since the previous November. But on their next trip over Germany, unloading five 1,000-pound bombs on the Focke-Wulf fighter factory at Bremen on April 17, they needed all their skills—along with the luck of tail gunner John Quinlan's horseshoe and the rabbit's foot carried by radioman Bob Hanson. A total of 16 of the bombers that took part in the Bremen mission were shot down. "Easily the greatest show I have ever seen," *Belle* copilot James Verinis noted in his diary, "flak from 200 guns and 150 fighters. What a trip."

Memphis Belle was said to be a lucky aircraft, but she had plenty of scars to show for it. Large portions of her tail had been shot off on two occasions. Engines had to be replaced nine times, along with both wings. The fuselage was so riddled with machine-gun and can-

Painted Personalities

Airmen not only named their planes, they also gave them personalities—in painted form. So-called nose art ranged from sexy to menacing. The Memphis Belle's famous lady (fuselage, opposite) was modeled on a "Petty Girl" (top right) created by artist George Petty for Esquire magazine, while the Flying Tigers—P-40s flown by Americans fighting for China early in the war—chose a fearsome look (right).

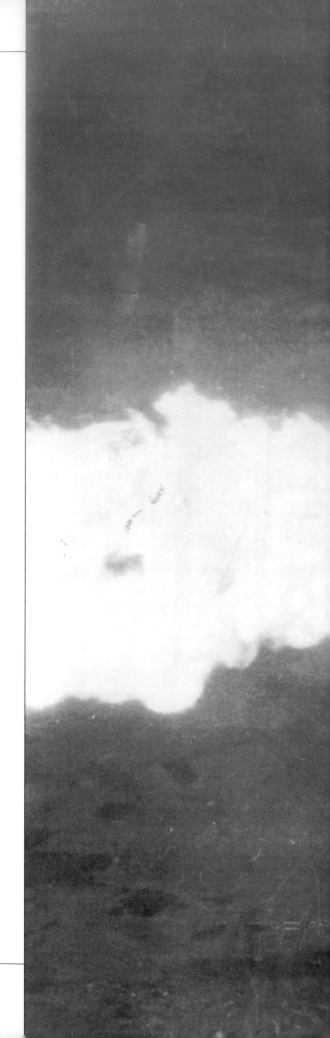

non holes that tail gunner Quinlan used one of the holes as an ashtray for his cigar butts. Yet no one had suffered a serious injury.

On May 17, Bob Morgan and his crew completed their 25th mission. When they returned from their target in France that day, Morgan— a maverick who liked to thumb his nose at the brass—buzzed the field so closely, it was alleged, that the flagpole atop headquarters toppled over. After landing, the men lifted Morgan on their shoulders so he could kiss the perky Memphis Belle pinup painted on the side of the plane. Eaker

then selected them to be honored as the first crew to fly 25 missions.

While the *Belle* and her crew flew back to the States for an official national tour to promote the war effort, their comrades kept flying and dying. By the end of May, no fewer than 188 U.S. bombers had been shot down over the Continent.

The Luftwaffe Fights Back. On August 17, 1943, the United States mounted its most ambitious effort yet—a double strike of more than 300 B-17s at two different cities deep in southeastern Germany. One force would hit the Messerschmitt fighter plant at Regensburg; the other would bomb the ball-bearing production complex at Schweinfurt. The double-barreled effort, it was hoped, would divide and overwhelm the German fighter defenses.

To reach Regensburg, the B-17s had to fly 300 miles over German territory without fighter protection. Their escorts, P-47 Thunderbolts, had such a short range that they were forced to turn back as soon as they reached the German border. That was when the Luftwaffe struck. Some 300 enemy interceptors, rising in relays from their bases, hounded the bombers all the way from the border to Regensburg. They attacked head-on and from above, firing machine guns, cannon, and, for the first time, rockets. Some of the interceptors even carried 500-pound bombs fused to explode in the midst of bomber formations. The bomber commander, a gruff 36-year-old Ohioan, Colonel Curtis LeMay, grumbled afterward that

Bombs spilling from its ruptured midsection, a B-24 Liberator bursts into flame over central Germany, the victim of antiaircraft fire from ground-based guns manned by the Luftwaffe. Besides flak, Allied bombers had to contend with squadrons of sleek Messerschmitt 109s (inset, above) and Focke-Wulf 190s—heavily armed interceptors that routinely decimated unescorted formations.

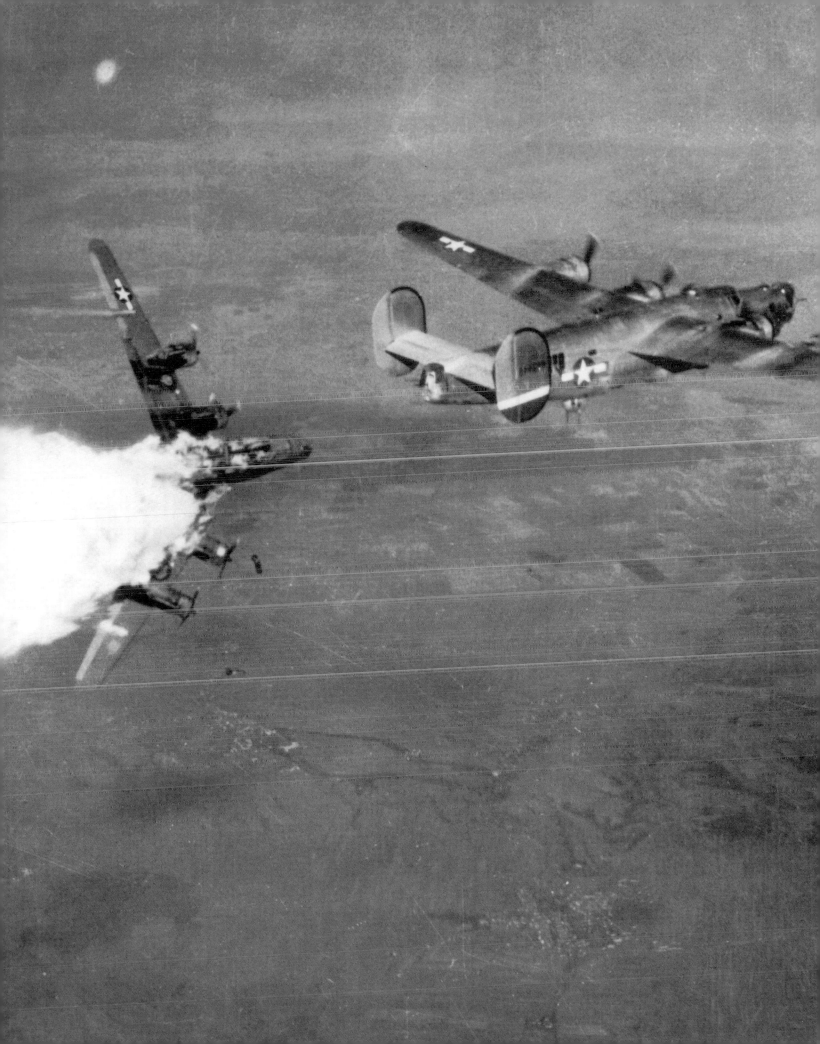

the only escorts he saw "had black crosses on their wings."

The second group of Flying Fortresses, bound for Schweinfurt, was supposed to take off only 10 minutes after the first wave of Regensburg raiders. But dense fog delayed takeoff by more than three hours. By that time the Luftwaffe fighters were refueled and rearmed. They would have a double shot at the Schweinfurt B-17s: Unlike the Regensburg bombers, which continued south after the attack to bases in North Africa, the second group had to run the gantlet of enemy fighters all the way from the German

border to Schweinfurt and then back again. Gunner Tom Murphy aboard the B-17 *Joker* was astonished to see German fighters so eager to get to the bombers that they were braving the flak from their own ground-based batteries. The total losses for the day were appalling. Of 376 B-17s dispatched in the double strike, 60 were shot down and 47 were so badly damaged they had to be scrapped.

The toll was even more devastating two months later when the Americans again targeted Schweinfurt. With all U.S. operations over Germany resulting in losses well

Tracing white contrails, fighters too distant to be seen escort B-17 bombers over France (left). Introduction of the P-51 Mustang (above) in 1944 provided protection all the way into Germany. Colonel Don Blakeslee (below) led his fighter pilots into combat after as little as 40 minutes of practice flying the Mustang.

"You can learn to fly them on the way to the target."

Colonel Don Blakeslee, 1944

above 10 percent, Eaker called off further major raids deep into the Reich, ordering that the bombers not return there in the daylight until they could be escorted all the way to the target and back by fighters.

Help was on the way. A powerful new Rolls Royce engine had transformed the P-51 Mustang, formerly a fighter intended for support of ground troops. It now had a speed of 440 mph and, thanks to remarkable fuel economy, the long range of a bomber. After Colonel Don Blakeslee tried out this new, improved Mustang, he promised to "have

them in combat in 24 hours" if his Fourth Fighter Group could get the aircraft. The 27-year-old Blakeslee already had flown 120 missions with the RAF during the Battle of Britain. He was so dedicated that he doctored his logbooks to prevent being rotated home, and so fiercely determined, according to one of his staff officers, that he "appeared to be made of cast iron laced together with steel cables."

Beginning in January 1944, Blakeslee led his Mustangs on escort missions against targets ever deeper into Germany. These "Little Friends"—radio parlance for escort fighters—quickly showed they could outrun, outdive, and outmaneuver the best German interceptors. The Mustangs were now joined by P-47 Thunderbolts, which enjoyed an extended range with the addition under their wings of a pair of auxiliary fuel tanks that could be dropped when empty. During the so-called Big Week—a six-day series of raids against the German aircraft industry—the escorts held bomber losses to under 7 percent.

With extra fuel tanks added to his Mustangs, Blakeslee could fly 1,200 miles—all the way to Berlin and back. He and his men did so on March 4 and 6 during the first U.S. bomber strikes against the German capital, which had been a frequent night objective of the RAF. Though costly, these missions demonstrated for the first time that the tide in the daylight air war had turned. Luftwaffe chief Hermann Göring said later that when he saw Mustangs over Berlin, "I knew the jig was up."

Destruction Day and Night. The growing armadas of bombers and fighters increasingly ruled the skies over Germany. Luftwaffe interceptors were virtually on the run as the marksmanship of Allied bomber gunners and the Little Friend escorts depleted their ranks; during the first four months of 1944, Germany lost 1,000 pilots in its day-fighter corps alone. Meanwhile, British and American bombers, now numbering up to 3,000 planes, struck almost at will by day and by night. Cities such as Hamburg *(right)* and Berlin were pulverized repeatedly, with rubble piling upon rubble. In all, an estimated 305,000 German civilians died in the bombing offensive. Even so, the terror from the sky did not crack the will of the Reich. Contrary to what Ira Eaker and other enthusiasts had believed, bombing alone would not defeat Germany; victory would have to be hard won on the ground.

But air power did make a decisive contribution in Europe. It allowed Allied ground troops to invade western Europe in June 1944 and then gradually penetrate the Reich itself. Thanks both to round-the-clock bombing and to the tactical air forces that directly supported the ground troops, the liberation of western Europe and the conquest of Germany would prove the prescience of the Allied supreme commander, General Dwight Eisenhower. On the eve of D-Day, he had told his troops, "If you see a plane, it will be one of ours."

In the burned-out medieval quarter of Hamburg, the ruins of Saint Nicholas Church (foreground) bear testimony to the destructive power of the Allied bombing offensive. Striking day and night in five raids during the summer of 1943, U.S. and British bombers ravaged 10 square miles of the city. Nearly 50,000 civilians died—a toll roughly equal to that suffered by England during all the raids by the Luftwaffe.

Flight decks laden with folded-wing fighters, torpedo planes, and dive bombers, two aircraft carriers head a lineup of battleships and cruisers steaming through the South Pacific. Launching and landing planes was organized mayhem during combat; at far right, a catapult officer gives the signal to launch an F6F Hellcat, the navy's premier fighter.

Pacific Seas, Pacific Skies

H alfway around the world from Europe, the air war was a quite different affair. In the Pacific theater permanent bases were rare, and planes frequently had to fly from improvised airstrips carved out of newly conquered little islands of coral and volcanic rock. But the most dramatic difference was the importance of the remarkable airfield that floated: the aircraft carrier. With nearly 100 aircraft aboard and flight decks up to almost 1,000 feet long to launch them, flattops could bring lethal force to bear on targets otherwise out of reach. Indeed, the devastating attack on December 7, 1941, that had brought the United States into the war had been made pos-

sible by six Japanese carriers coming to within 200 miles of Pearl Harbor. For the U.S., the blow was mitigated only by the fact that its own carriers had been safely elsewhere during the attack.

History's first duel between carriers occurred five months later in the Coral Sea, off the southern tip of New Guinea. Learning via a radio message that the Japanese were sending a carrier-escorted invasion force to Port Moresby, the United States dispatched four carriers. On May 7, 1942, planes from the *Lexington* and the *Yorktown* sank the light carrier *Shoho*. The next day, the Japanese retaliated by crippling the *Lexington,* which had to be abandoned and scuttled. The Battle of the Coral Sea was the first time ships had fought without coming into visual contact or exchanging gunfire. A tactical standoff, it nonetheless forced Japan to call off the invasion of Port Moresby—the first check in its southward expansion.

The Japanese naval commander, Admiral Isoroku Yamamoto, then hatched a plan to destroy the U.S. carrier

Its home carrier presents a tiny target for a Helldiver dive bomber turning in for a landing on what was often a pitching deck. Like the earlier Dauntless, the Helldiver had a two-man crew; during bombing runs, the gunner in the rear cockpit provided some protection against the ubiquitous Japanese Zero (opposite).

force. One flotilla would attack the Aleutian Islands off Alaska as a diversion while a much larger force covered a landing on Midway. A tiny U.S.-occupied island roughly halfway between the North American continent and Asia, Midway lay some 1,150 miles northwest of Pearl Harbor. The invasion of this strategically located island, Yamamoto believed, would lure the U.S. carriers and enable his planes to blast them out of the water.

As at Coral Sea, the Americans got wind of the plan through a radio intercept. Early on the morning of June 4, 1942, their carriers were waiting 325 miles northeast of Midway. The Japanese carriers were preoccupied with strikes against the garrison on Midway and had no idea of the American naval presence. A U.S. reconnaissance plane from Midway spotted the enemy carriers and alerted the American flattops.

The first wave launched by the Americans consisted of three squadrons of Devastator torpedo bombers. These obsolete craft, with a top speed of only 200 mph, were escorted by F4F Wildcat fighters. The Wildcat's job was to hold off the Japanese Zero—the Mitsubishi A6M, Type O fighter (above, right). Lightweight and agile, the Zero could fly faster, higher, and farther than the fighters it faced, and it could outmaneuver them as well. The Zeroes pounced on the low-flying torpedo planes, firing machine guns and cannon. All three U.S. torpedo squadrons were virtually wiped out. The worst hit, Squadron 8, which had become separated from its Wildcat escorts, lost all 15 planes. The squadron's lone surviving pilot, Ensign George "Tex" Gay, ditched his crippled bomber and clung to a floating seat cushion. Bobbing amid the Japanese ships, he had an uncomfortably closeup view of the spectacular show that followed.

While Tex Gay tried to hide behind his cushion (he was later rescued), four U.S. squadrons of sturdy and reliable Dauntless dive bombers began their attacks. The Japanese Zeroes, flying low to meet the torpedo bombers, were caught off guard. One by one, the American dive bombers peeled off at an altitude of 14,500 feet and hurtled down at 275 mph. At 2,000 feet, each pilot let loose his single bomb and then wrenched up his craft's nose. In rapid succession, bombs struck three Japanese carriers—the *Kaga, Akagi,* and *Soryu.* On the flight decks and below, the hits detonated bombs and torpedoes and ignited volatile aviation fuel. In minutes, flames were leaping from all three carriers.

Soon dive bombers from the fourth Japanese carrier, *Hiryu,* caught up with some of the attacking planes. Following them back to the carrier

Relentless Enemy Ace

Japan's leading ace, Saburo Sakai, personified his nation's air superiority in the early days of the Pacific war and its grim determination thereafter. Sakai considered the Mitsubishi Zero (top) "a dream to fly," and by August 1942 he had used it to shoot down 60 enemy planes. Then he lost an eye in aerial combat near Guadalcanal and was made a flight instructor. Desperate for pilots, Japan returned him to combat in 1944, by which time his beloved Zero had become obsolete—overtaken by improved U.S. fighters that took advantage of its lack of armor and a self-sealing fuel tank. But Sakai fought on and, despite his impaired vision, scored five more kills, including the very last B-29 shot down in the war.

Nearing the bottom of its dive, a U.S. Dauntless dive bomber releases a 500-pound bomb. Perforated brakes on the wings enabled the pilot to hold his diving speed at a steady 275 mph.

A hail of antiaircraft fire envelops a Japanese torpedo bomber headed in on an attack run. Seconds after this photo was taken, the ship's gunners shot down the intruder.

Yorktown, they scored three direct hits. Firefighters had the blazes under control when, in midafternoon, torpedo planes from the *Hiryu* arrived and sent a pair of torpedoes into the port side. Listing dangerously, the *Yorktown* had to be abandoned.

The Japanese attackers had scarcely returned to the *Hiryu* when American planes appeared overhead. Two dozen dive bombers launched by the *Enterprise*— more than half of them refugees from the abandoned *Yorktown*—roared down and unloaded their 1,000-pound bombs. Four slammed home on the airplane-laden flight deck and set it ablaze. Before the *Hiryu* was abandoned later that night, Admiral Tamon Yamaguchi, the brilliant chief of air operations, addressed the crew in the light of the burning flight deck: He took full responsibility and would go down with the ship. Then he ordered one of his nearby destroyers, "Torpedo and sink the *Hiryu.*" A few hours later, the Japanese canceled their scheduled invasion of Midway.

The Battle of Midway had cost the Japanese four carriers, 234 planes, and 2,500 lives, including 100 of their most experienced pilots. The U.S. losses were one carrier, 147 planes, and 307 men. The Imperial Navy had been dealt a blow from which it would never recover. To Lieutenant Richard Best, whose dive bomber helped cripple the *Akagi,* Midway "was revenge for the humiliation of Pearl Harbor."

The U.S. carrier Franklin erupts in flame and flying debris after being hit by a Japanese dive bomber in early 1945. The bombing caused 724 deaths, but the ship survived to be repaired.

Taking the Islands

When he took command of the U.S. Fifth Air Force in the summer of 1942, Major General George Kenney wanted "air control so supreme that the birds have to wear our Air Force insignia." Kenney's men had the job of supporting the westward advance of General Douglas MacArthur along the rugged 1,200-mile-long northern coast of New Guinea. Before each infantry attack, bombers and fighters pounded Japanese troops. Kenney fostered innovative low-altitude techniques, putting extra guns on bombers to strafe enemy ground positions and parachutes on bombs so his low-flying planes could get out of harm's way before the explosion.

Once an area was secured, new airstrips were constructed, and the Fifth Air Force leapfrogged forward to attack the next enemy enclave. In addition, C-47 transports ferried in troops and supplies and dropped paratroopers to bypass enemy strongpoints. Thus aided, MacArthur moved northwest from New Guinea and made good his promise to return to the Philippines.

Meanwhile, the Seventh Air Force supported the island-hopping campaign in the central Pacific. Perilous and tedious work—"one damned island after another," complained the aircrews—their efforts helped bring air power to the brink of its most persuasive application: the bombing of Japan's home islands.

America's "Bad Boy" Hero

During training in the U.S., he had to be reprimanded for buzzing so low he blew the wash off a clothesline. But in New Guinea, Richard Bong, "that stunt-flying bad boy," was Major General George Kenney's first choice for a new fighter squadron formed in the fall of 1942. It flew the P-38 Lightning, a swift, twin-engine interceptor that climbed, Bong said, "like a homesick angel." Lightnings shot down more Japanese planes than any other U.S. fighter—and Bong had more than his share of hits. A mediocre marksman, he scored by swooping down on his target and blasting away before pulling up at the last minute to avoid collision. In 146 missions, he amassed 40 kills to become America's highest-scoring ace. Ordered home for his own protection, he died less than a month before the end of the war in the crash of a new jet fighter he was testing.

Skirting the treetops, a B-25 Mitchell bomber strafes Japanese antiaircraft gun positions on New Guinea in 1943. Fifth Air Force B-25s were custom-fitted with up to 10 forward-facing machine guns for low-flying ground attacks.

Mission: Japan

By early 1945 everything seemed to be in place. The Americans had the necessary forward airfields on recently conquered islands. They had the newest bomber in the form of the B-29 Superfortress *(left)*. And they had tough, innovative leadership in Major General Curtis LeMay *(inset, with pipe)*, a European veteran so demanding that he had been known to his men there as Iron Ass. The mission: Wage an all-out bombing assault against the Japanese homeland.

Bombing Japan had been on the minds of U.S. airmen since very early in the war. In April 1942—only four months after Pearl Harbor—the Army Air Corps teamed up with the navy for a token raid to bolster morale and remind the Japanese  they did not live beyond the reach of war. Sailing within 750 miles of Tokyo, the carrier *Hornet* launched 16 B-25 Mitchell bombers led by Lieutenant Colonel Jimmy Doolittle. The B-25s hit Tokyo and three other Japanese cities.

When B-29s became available in the spring of 1944, they first operated against Japan from newly constructed airstrips in central China. With its centralized gun-control system, extended range, and pressurized compartments, the Superfortress represented a big improvement over its predecessors. But flying it from China was a logistical nightmare. Gasoline had to be flown in from bases in India over the 23,000-foot-high section of the Himalayas known as the Hump, and it took six B-29s to carry enough fuel in 55-gallon drums for a single Superfortress sortie. Even then the bombers could reach only as far as Kyushu, Japan's

---

At a new bomber base on Guam, a bulldozer clears away stumps while, in the background, a maintenance crew services a B-29. Airstrips on Pacific islands were typically carved out of the jungle, with runways fashioned from pulverized coral. This and other bases in the Marianas put bombers within striking range of Japan.

In the bomb bay of a B-29 (left), an ordnance man inserts a propeller fuse into a high-explosive bomb. At right, as incendiary bombs explode over the city of Sakai in July 1945, a B-29 is caught in the cross beams of Japanese searchlights.

westernmost island. The first raid from China on June 15, 1944, was all too typical of the handful that followed: Just one bomb hit the overall target, a large steelworks, and it landed more than a half-mile from the aiming point.

Beginning in November 1944, the new bases in the Marianas allowed the B-29s to strike regularly at virtually all of Japan, but the results disappointed U.S. planners. Like the bombing campaign against Germany, these raids were high-altitude daylight precision attacks aimed at specific targets such as aircraft factories. Over Japan, however, clouds consistently obscured targets, and at 30,000 feet, where the B-29s flew, jet-stream winds kept blowing the big bombers off course.

Even after LeMay took command at the end of January 1945, losses were high and the bombing damage inconsequential. At the suggestion of superiors, he tried switching to area bombing with incendiary devices, then came up with some changes that turned conventional doctrine upside down: Bomb at night

---

"Japan has sowed the wind. Now let it reap the whirlwind."

General Henry "Hap" Arnold, commanding general of the
U.S. Army Air Forces

---

like the British RAF in Germany to reduce the opposition from interceptors. Bomb at low altitudes to get under the cloud cover and strong winds and to increase accuracy. Bomb with more bombs, doubling the payload per plane, by leaving three of the crew and their guns at home to decrease weight. "If this works the way I think it will," he told his skeptical staff, "we can shorten this war."

It worked even more effectively than LeMay had envisioned. In the first test of the new tactics on the night of March 9, 1945, 334 B-29s headed for Tokyo. Flying as low as 5,000 feet over the city, they unleashed magnesium bombs that

A plummeting kamikaze plane barely misses the plane-crowded deck of the escort carrier Sanga-mon in May 1945. Pilots selected for suicide missions often were raw recruits with less than 30 hours of training. Some kamikaze candidates were so eager to die for their country that they wrote their applications in blood.

Ready for the supreme sacrifice, kamikaze pilots (opposite) gather for a last portrait before takeoff. Suicide pilots were honored as heirs to the samurai warrior tradition. One of them wrote his parents, "I have been given a splendid opportunity to die."

burned with a white heat and clusters of other incendiaries filled with the jellied gasoline napalm. The firestorm was so intense that the city's canal water boiled over, and the up-drafts bounced "our planes into the sky like ping-pong balls," LeMay wrote later. Nearly 16 square miles of the city was reduced to ashes, and more than 80,000 Japanese died.

Thus began the incineration of urban Japan: Nagoya, Osaka, and Kobe. Japanese air defenses were powerless to stop the fire raids. Their fighters were ineffective at night, and their antiaircraft guns lacked the aid of radar. LeMay had found the key to bombing Japan, and he wanted to "bomb and burn them until they quit."

The Kamikaze Menace. Less than a month into the fire raids, LeMay's B-29s were temporarily given another mis-sion: daylight attacks against airfields on the Japanese is-lands of Kyushu and Shikoku. These were the bases of the kamikaze suicide pilots who deliberately crashed their bomb-laden aircraft into U.S. ships. Named for the "divine wind" typhoons that twice had turned back Mongol-led Chinese invaders during the 13th century, the kamikazes had begun operations against American carriers and other ships five months earlier. Fanatically determined to be the divine wind that would stave off the Americans, they had become a serious menace.

During April, the Superfortresses pummeled more than a score of kamikaze bases, but the kamikazes simply camouflaged their planes and kept them off the airstrips. Then they struck with mass suicide attacks of 300 or more aircraft—old Zero fighters, Val dive bombers, even trainers. Some 1,900 kamikazes sacrificed their lives during the two-month-long *kikusui*, or "floating chrysanthemums," campaign around Okinawa, sink-ing 29 U.S. ships and killing more than 5,000 sailors.

LeMay resumed full-scale fire raids in May 1945, and by August he was running out of major targets. He was now targeting small cities of un-der 40,000 and shrewdly creating panic by dropping leaflets that warned of an impending attack even if it would be directed elsewhere. That sum-mer he had 1,000 Superfortresses at hand and fighter escorts available when needed from the P-51 Mustangs based on Okinawa and Iwo Jima.

It was enough, LeMay firmly believed, to finish off the enemy. His su-periors were far less certain. The fanaticism demonstrated by the kamikazes

After returning from Hiroshima, the crew of the B-29 Enola Gay meets on Tinian Island. Their commander, Colonel Paul Tibbets Jr. (center), had his mother's name painted on the bomber's nose.

Hiroshima—untouched by raids earlier—lies devastated after the atomic attack. The bomb was targeted on the bridge at right; ground zero was 300 yards off, to the left of one of the few remaining buildings.

and Japanese ground troops on Okinawa suggested that the homeland would be similarly defended. An invasion of Japan was being planned for November, and some strategists feared it might cost up to one million American casualties.

Two Bombs to End the War. Hoping to avoid the high price in lives that an invasion would exact, U.S. strategists had in mind a different kind of mission for the B-29— one involving a wholly different kind of weapon. The pilots and crews for this top-secret project arrived in the Marianas that summer under the command of Colonel Paul Tibbets Jr., a 30-year-old veteran of Europe and North Africa. LeMay's bomber crews griped about the newcomers, labeling them a "bunch of pampered dandies" because they flew only special training missions. The components for the mysterious weapon were delivered by the cruiser *Indianapolis*, which—not a happy omen—was sunk by a Japanese submarine three days later. The weapon had been secretly

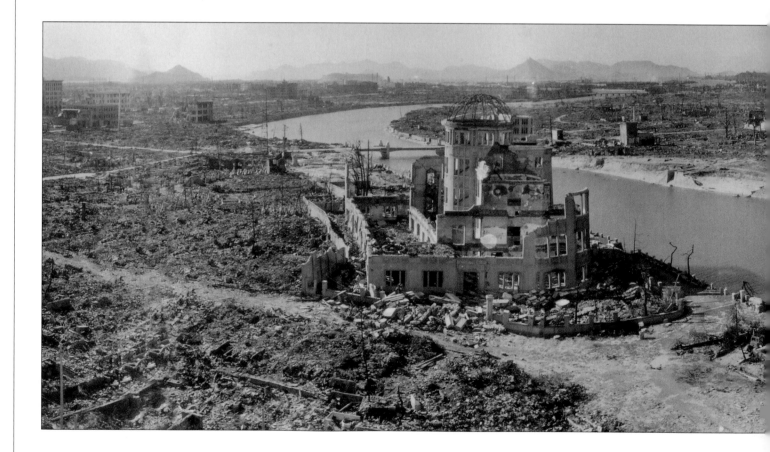

tested in the New Mexico desert and its use against Japan authorized at the highest level by President Harry S Truman.

At 2:45 a.m. on August 6, 1945, Tibbets and his crew took off in the B-29 he had named *Enola Gay* after his mother. Soon a naval ordnance specialist, Captain William Parsons, crawled into the cramped bomb bay and armed the weapon, which was a metal cylinder 10 feet long and 20 inches in diameter, code-named Little Boy. He had waited until the plane was airborne to make the weapon ready for use because B-29s were notorious for crashing during take-off. Only when Tibbets learned that the weapon was fully armed did he switch on the intercom and, after months of evasion, disclose to the crew the nature of the weapon: "We are carrying the world's first atomic bomb."

The target was Hiroshima, a city of 245,000 that had escaped the worst of the fire raids. At 8:15 a.m., from an altitude of 31,600 feet, the *Enola Gay* released the world's first operational atomic bomb and then

Radioactive steam, dust, and ash billows above Hiroshima. The cloud rose 20,000 feet within the first minute after detonation.

broke hard to the right, dropped its nose, and gathered speed to escape. Some 50 seconds later, the bomb exploded about 1,885 feet above the city with such force that people standing near ground zero had their shadows burned into the concrete. Tail gunner George Caron saw the mushroom-shaped cloud rising to the level of the plane like "a mass of bubbling molasses." Nearly five square miles of the city was obliterated that day, and an estimated 140,000 people died then and later. Only after a second atomic attack—three days later on the city of Nagasaki—did the Japanese government agree to surrender.

The ceremony formalizing the surrender took place on September 2, 1945, aboard the battleship *Missouri*. Air power was prominently represented. The dramatic flyover *(right)* at the end of the ceremony included 462 B-29s, the Superfortresses that had delivered the final decisive and terrible blows upon Japan.

"We have learned how to win a war in this air age. Our best hope for a long and secure peace lies in remembering what we have learned."

Robert A. Lovett,
Assistant Secretary of War for Air

In a massive display of Allied air power, an armada of 1,900 planes fills the sky over Tokyo Bay on September 2, 1945, to salute the formal surrender ceremonies on the battleship Missouri (left foreground).

Something New Under the Sun

★

JETS COME OF AGE

When it first came screaming out of European skies in the fall of 1944, Allied pilots thought they were hallucinating. The thing was a plane, to be sure—but with its primitive, sharklike contours, no propeller, and breathtaking speed, it was like nothing they had ever seen. Instantly, their piston-driven airplanes seemed as antiquated as Model Ts.

The secret behind Germany's Me 262—the world's first operational jet fighter—was its gas-turbine engine, whose exhaust acted like air escaping from a balloon to power the craft at speeds of more than 550 mph. Luftwaffe pilots who flew it never looked back. "It was as though angels were pushing," marveled Adolf Galland, chief of the German fighter force.

A few Allied pilots dared to challenge this new creature. One was a wiry 21-year-old from West Virginia named Chuck Yeager. From the cockpit of his prop-driven P-51 Mustang, Yeager brought down a 262 while it was landing. "The first time I ever saw a jet, I shot it down," Yeager said later.

That matter-of-fact attitude came to typify pilots of the jet age. Whether they were testing the limits in experimental craft—as Yeager himself would do *(right)*—or flying commercial jetliners, time and again it was keeping cool that counted most.

Aglow in the sun's slanting rays, Chuck Yeager stands beside the X-1, the world's first supersonic plane. Named for Yeager's wife, the Glamorous Glennis (inset) was painted orange to be seen more easily.

Ma Green's Cafe (above) was a favorite hangout for airmen from Muroc Army Air Base during the 1940s. They had few other choices.

If they weren't at Ma's, they'd be at the piano at Pancho's (above). Chuck Yeager (next to Pancho) and fellow test pilot Jack Ridley (far left) were regulars at the hacienda-like ranch (below).

Supersonic: The Fast Life at Muroc

Muroc Army Air Base was a desolate place, next to a dry lake bed in California's Mojave Desert. The only action in town—not that there was a town—was at a ranch out beyond the end of the runway that served as bar, officers' club, and all-around party joint. Pancho Barnes, a hotshot pilot in her own right, was the mistress of ceremonies, and she knew that those flyboys from Muroc needed to unwind just as much as they needed to stay sharp. They were putting their necks on the line every day, not to win a war, but to prove what jets could do.

Pancho Barnes in 1929

The United States had been developing the jet for several years, and its first—the Airacomet—had flown in 1942, at a relatively modest top speed of about 400 mph. But with higher speeds came problems, one of which was recognized with propeller planes during the war: During high-speed dives, fighters had a tendency to disintegrate. Without

Club membership card

ground test facilities to simulate the conditions, the only way to resolve such issues was to construct a specialized research aircraft. So, in 1944 the Army Air Forces (AAF) contracted Bell Aircraft to build a rocket-powered plane, designated the XS-1 (for experimental-sonic), that could travel faster than the speed of sound—mach 1, a speed upward of 650 mph that varies with the air's temperature. It was not an arbitrary target. At speeds approaching mach 1, theoreticians knew that so-called compressibility effects—

disruptions of airflow caused by pressure-shock waves—made an aircraft difficult to control; although no one knew for sure, the assumption was that compressibility effects at the speed of sound could destroy a plane or cause so much drag that the "barrier" would never be broken.

Conquering this potentially unconquerable challenge required patient, careful research and design adjustments by engineers at Bell, working closely with the AAF and the National Advisory Committee for Aeronautics (NACA). By autumn 1946, Bell had produced an aircraft ready for powered flight. Muroc was chosen for the tests primarily because the surrounding desert flats left plenty of room for error. To conserve fuel, the XS-1 was to be carried under the belly of a B-29 bomber and drop-launched. Its rocket engine—producing exhaust thrust like a jet engine, but by burning propellant fuel, not by sucking in and expelling air via a spinning turbine—would then fire. A series of flights was planned, each one closer to mach 1.

Dancing at Pancho's

Test pilot Chalmers "Slick" Goodlin, a civilian working for Bell, flew the first tests, reaching mach .8. Unfortunately for him, contractual difficulties led to a decision to use an AAF pilot, and Chuck Yeager replaced Goodlin.

Unlike other test pilots with engineering degrees, Yeager had only a high-school diploma. But he had an intuitive grasp of flight dynamics and, having shot down 12 German planes during the war, had a reputation for being tough.

Part of his secret was knowing how to blow off steam, and Pancho's—now called the Happy Bottom Riding Club—was the place for that. A wealthy heiress and ex-Hollywood stunt pilot, Florence "Pancho" Barnes had run guns for Mexican revolutionaries, took the women's air speed record from Amelia Earhart, and had a tongue that shocked the most hard-boiled cynic. She was just what the doctor ordered. Around her tinny piano, members of the

Pancho's ranch (above) was close enough to Muroc's main runway that pilots would frequently buzz it on takeoff—and some claimed that their wheels actually scraped the rooftops. The ranch burned in 1953, and the land was cleared for a longer runway.

Yeager and his wife, Glennis, share a moment with their children at their home on the base. Conditions for families were difficult, and there was always that fear of something happening to Dad.

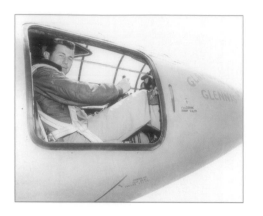

"Yeager, this is Ridley. You all set?"
"Hell yes, let's get it over with."

Radio exchange before the X-1's historic flight

brotherhood-elect staggered through Cole Porter tunes and mingled with luscious hostesses, much to the chagrin of their wives. Good-natured brawling over who was the best test pilot was common; the loser usually was thrown into Pancho's swimming pool. As Yeager put it, "Flying and hell-raising—one fueled the other. . . . That's what Pancho's was all about."

Letting off steam wasn't the only reason Yeager was able to keep his cool before the sound barrier. The Mustang he flew during World War II had fired .50-caliber bullets that were known to "fly" in a stable flight and not tumble; the research plane in which he would assault the sound barrier was shaped just like those bullets, with a needle nose. Also, the X-1 (the S had been dropped) had razor-thin wings to pierce shock waves. In need of a good-luck charm, Yeager named the plane *Glamorous Glennis* after his wife and had the letters painted across its bright orange nose.

Yeager made a series of powered flights in the X-1, with program engineers working out airflow problems along the way with adjustments to the plane's unique "flying tail," a design feature originally suggested by NACA. His ninth flight was scheduled for October 14, and the plan called for a top speed of mach .96 only.

If everything had gone by the book, Yeager would never have made that flight. Two nights before, he went with Glennis for a midnight gallop at Pancho's. Racing back to the corral, he failed to see that the gate was shut, flew over his horse's head, and cracked two ribs. He kept mum about it, but he couldn't use his arm to shut the door in the X-1's cockpit. So on the morning of October 14, flight engineer Jack Ridley slipped him part of a broom handle, allowing him enough leverage to close the door with his good arm.

Yeager, with his broken ribs, climbed into the B-29's bomb bay. At 7,000 feet he descended a ladder, squeezed into the cockpit, and shut the door with a shove of his broom handle. At 20,000 feet, the mother ship released her baby. As Yeager fired his four rocket chambers one by one he shot up to 42,000 feet, then leveled off. The machmeter needle climbed, reached .965, wavered, and tipped off the scale. Yeager was supersonic. (Observers on the ground heard the world's first aircraft sonic boom.) After some buffeting, the transition had been so smooth, he said later, that "Grandma could be sitting up there sipping lemonade."

With a side panel of the X-1 removed, Yeager shows how cramped the cockpit was (top). The X-1 team, who autographed the photograph above in 1947, included (left to right) Ed Swindell, Bob Hoover, Bob Cardenas, Yeager, Dick Frost, and Jack Ridley, who was also the overall project engineer.

Mach 1 Is Not Enough. The story was far from over with Yeager's success. Faster was always better, and eventually the target became mach 2,

Having broken the sound barrier, the X-1 leaves behind a shock wave as it speeds over the test range. Its four-chambered rocket engine generated an astonishing 6,000 total pounds of thrust.

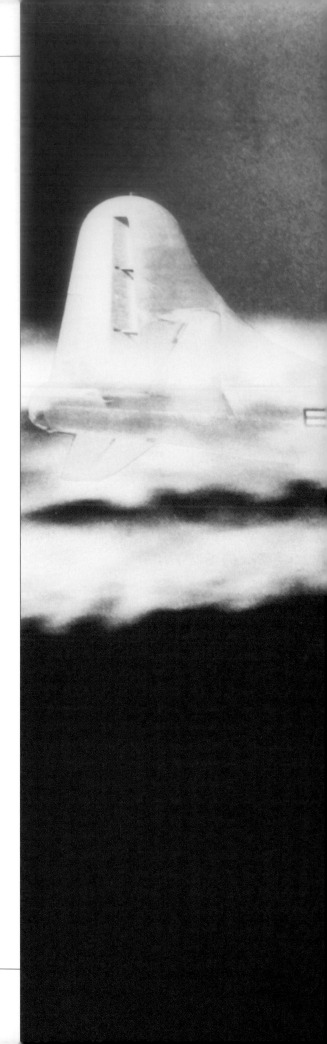

twice the speed of sound. Across the windblown stretches of Muroc—now renamed Edwards Air Force Base—an intense rivalry heated up between two services and two very different men: Yeager, the natural-born ace flying the new X-1A for the air force (formerly the Army Air Forces), and NACA research pilot A. Scott Crossfield (below), an aeronautical engineer flying the navy's Douglas D-558-2 Skyrocket.

The 50th anniversary of the Wright brothers' flight brought the competition to a head. A commemorative dinner was planned for December 1953, and the air force was hoping to unveil Yeager as the first man to conquer both mach 1 and mach 2. Few expected the Skyrocket to challenge for mach 2, but Crossfield thought there was a chance. "Wouldn't it be nice if we could whip Yeager's ass?" he hinted to his superiors, who agreed to let him try. Crossfield had his NACA crew do all they could to coax a few extra knots out of the aircraft, including polishing and waxing it and chilling the alcohol fuel, which increased its density and enabled the plane to carry more. On November 20, 1953, the Skyrocket was drop-launched at 32,000 feet. Crossfield hit his rocket switches and, guiding the ship through a near-perfect parabola, surged up to 72,000 feet, pushed over, and began a spectacular downhill run. As he watched, elated, the machmeter edged to 2.005.

Yeager was not to be outdone, even though some of the engineers were uneasy about the X-1A's handling at speeds greater than mach 2. On December 12, just days before the memorial dinner, Yeager went blasting skyward and at 74,000 feet reached mach 2.44. Then, as feared, the X-1A "uncorked" and came tumbling out of the sky. Dropping 51,000 feet in 51 seconds, the plane slammed Yeager around like a rag doll, and he lapsed into semiconsciousness. When all seemed lost, he managed to get the plane into a normal spin, a situation from which he knew how to recover. It was the fastest, wildest ride in aviation history—and Yeager had pulled through. Crossfield was the first pilot to crack mach 2, but at the Wright brothers memorial dinner it was his air force rival who was showered with accolades and the unofficial title of Fastest Man Alive.

Scott Crossfield, who beat Yeager in the race for mach 2, later flew the record-setting X-15 (page 165).

One of the navy's Skyrockets fires its engine just after drop-launching from the B-29 mother ship. The sweptwing aircraft was originally designed to take off from the ground with both jet and rocket engines but was modified for air-launching and full rocket power to increase its speed.

Test pilot A. M. "Tex" Johnston, shown here before the 707 prototype's first flight, said later, "The airplane was a dream . . . quiet and vibration free."

Flying the Commercial Skies

One test pilot who had flown both the Airacomet and the X-1 was A. M. "Tex" Johnston. In his youth a barnstormer for a flying circus, Johnston had a flare for drama. As Boeing's chief test pilot, he was asked to put the company's prototype 707 through its paces before a crowd assembled along Seattle's Lake Washington for the Gold Cup Hydroplane Boat races on August 7, 1955. Boeing had much at stake. Its president, Bill Allen, had gambled $15 million on a single prototype in the hope that airline companies would flock to him with orders for his company's first commercial jet—a big "if." British de Havilland had recently grounded its pioneering Comet jetliners after a series of tragic accidents. No matter how fast, quiet, or silky

smooth a ride jets offered, it would be difficult to reassure the public about the safety of this new mode of travel.

The Dash 80, as the prototype was called, had a fuselage eight feet longer than the distance flown by Wilbur Wright on the first powered flight. At the appointed time, Johnston took this huge $15 million gamble into a shallow dive over Lake Washington. Before several hundred thousand spectators—including Allen and his guest, Bell Aircraft president Larry Bell—Tex executed a full barrel roll, then went into another dive and repeated the stunt. Allen was aghast. Larry Bell just laughed. "Bill," he quipped, "he just sold your airplane."

On October 26, 1958, the 707 made its inaugural flight as Pan Am's Clipper America, carrying a record 111 passen-

Boeing's 707 prototype, the Dash 80, set the stage for the boom in jet travel; the 1959 advertisement at top noted a milestone.

"Just after landing, with its nose still down, it might be some prehistoric monster with curious eating habits."

Former Concorde pilot Brian Calvert

The Concorde, which cruises at twice the speed of sound, blends functionality with a sleek, aesthetic form. The sweptback wings delicately balance the needs of both high- and low-speed flight, and during takeoff and landing the hinged nose dips down to improve visibility for pilots.

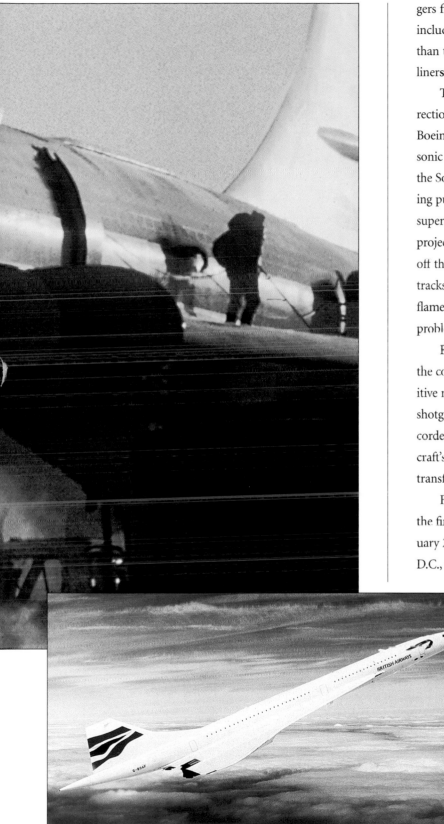

gers from New York to Paris. With nearly fail-safe features, including an aluminum skin four and a half times thicker than the ill-fated Comet's, it was one of the strongest airliners ever to come out of production.

The future of jet travel was now assured, if not its direction. Some pushed for sleeker, faster jetliners. In 1966 Boeing, with U.S. government funding, launched a supersonic transport (SST) project, spurred in part by fear that the Soviets had a head start in this field. But in 1971 mounting public fear over the possible environmental effects of supersonic flight, not to mention the exorbitant cost of the project—three billion dollars before the first SST even came off the production line—stopped the U.S. effort dead in its tracks. Two years later a Soviet SST erupted in a ball of flame at the Paris Air Show, demonstrating one of many problems that eventually killed the Communist program.

Back in 1962, hoping to capture a market niche from the colossal American aircraft industry, the fiercely competitive nations of Britain and France had joined hands in a shotgun wedding to produce an SST of their own, the Concorde. Soon enough, skyrocketing investment costs, the aircraft's hefty appetite for fuel, and limited passenger seating transformed this promising hope into a white elephant.

Fourteen years after the joint program was launched, the first two Concordes entered commercial service on January 21, 1976. The sleek jets could cruise from Washington, D.C., to Paris in three and a half hours—less than half the usual time—while a machmeter mounted on the cabin wall displayed their thrilling speed. Customers loved the plane. One executive for a Tennessee pencil company flew it 63 times. Still, supersonic flight was limited mostly to people on expense accounts, and airline companies were hard pressed to sell tickets. Three years after inaugural day, the partners divorced with a measly 16 planes completed. The Concorde was the costliest, most disappointing airliner ever built.

Captain Al Haynes received lavish praise for bringing his crippled DC-10 in for a near-level landing and avoiding total disaster. Those who survived credited him with saving their lives.

"You want to be particular and make it a runway? I'm just aiming for Iowa."

Haynes, after being cleared for landing

The wreckage of Flight 232 burns in a cornfield next to the runway. Rows 9 to 19 were the only part of the main passenger cabin to remain intact.

The other trend in commercial development was the subsonic jumbo jet. American airline companies had long ago learned that the way to turn a profit was to widen a plane's body and squeeze in as many seats as possible. By the early 1970s airlines were flying jumbo jets that carried over three times the number of passengers in the old Pan Am Clipper America.

A Day for Heroes. Accidents on these crowded widebodies, though rare, could be shockingly tragic. Such was the case with United Airlines DC-10 Flight 232. Yet thanks to the nerve and expertise of pilot Al Haynes, out of that tragedy came a small miracle.

On July 19, 1989, Flight 232 was en route from Denver to Chicago when passengers felt a jolt and heard an explosion coming from the tail. With a shudder, the plane pitched down. Engine number two was out, a member of the flight crew calmly told the passengers. They would be arriving late in Chicago.

It would take Haynes a few minutes more to register the severity of the explosion. Metal shards had gone ripping through three hydraulic lines that powered the steering controls. With one chance in a billion that all three lines would fail, he and his crew had no contingency plan—and apparently no way to steer. In a desperate attempt to guide the craft down for an emergency landing in Sioux City, Iowa, Haynes resorted to a tricky maneuver: alternating the thrust on his two wing-mounted engines. An off-duty United instructor pilot, Dennis Fitch, arrived in the cockpit to manipulate the engine throttles while Haynes and copilot William Records wrestled with the wheel. Making wide right turns, the plane wobbled toward runway 22. "Brace! Brace! Brace!" Haynes barked over the intercom.

Remarkably, most passengers remained calm. The plane appeared to be making a steady approach. Then, 10 seconds short of the runway, its right wing sliced into the earth and sent the DC-10 cartwheeling across the runway. Severed from the nose, the center fuselage skidded across the tarmac and dead-ended upside down in a field of sweet Iowa corn.

At the end of the 41-minute ordeal 112 people were dead. But amazingly, 184 lived. Rescue crews were dumbfounded by the sight of survivors stumbling through tall waves of corn in the eerie silence of a brilliant Iowa day. All the men in the cockpit lived—the first aircrew in history to survive total loss of steering control in a commercial plane. They had proved that no matter how mundane it might sometimes seem, piloting airplanes was still a job for heroes.

A National Guardsman carries one of the plane's youngest passengers to safety. When the plane's nose snapped off, it left one end of the passenger cabin open, easing rescue work.

Hot Wars and Cold

★

STAYING ON TOP IN THE AIR

On April 26, 1953, two B-29 bombers dropped a million leaflets near the banks of North Korea's Yalu River. A hefty reward, they announced, would go to any Communist pilot who delivered a Soviet-made MiG-15 into American hands. Five months later, a plane that fit the description came rolling down a runway near Seoul. The pilot got his reward—and the Americans their first close look at the jet that had both alarmed and fascinated them ever since its debut back in 1948.

The nimble, elusive MiG would surface time and again over the next five decades in various updated versions, inspiring Americans to produce faster, more agile fighters and bull's-eye weapons. Cold War tensions speeded the development of supersecret spy planes and the huge, long-range bombers of the Strategic Air Command *(insignia, left),* fleets of which cruised the skies 24 hours a day, ever ready with the deterrent threat of their nuclear arsenals.

Through the years, technological advances continued to change warplanes—and the role of the pilot. From the first electronically controlled fly-by-wire jets of the 1970s to state-of-the-art stealth fighters and bombers, aviators were constantly learning to handle machines with reflexes infinitely better than their own. The best fliers only got better as a result—and the century-long partnership between plane and pilot only grew stronger.

Banking sharply to the right, an F-16 pilot displays some of the agility of modern fly-by-wire fighters. The F-16 was the first U.S. warplane to replace mechanical connections with speed-of-light electronics.

Two U.S. pilots head for their jets and for MiG Alley—the region along North Korea's Chinese border that was prime territory for hunting down the Russian-built fighters.

Jets Over Korea

Early in November 1950, an escort of America's first operational jets, F-80 Shooting Stars, was hovering watchfully above a B-29 bombing fleet as it lay waste to the North Korean city of Sinuiju. Out of the blue, six MiG-15s swooped down on the escort and let go a shower of cannon fire. As their tracers scattered to the winds, five of the MiGs zipped back across the Yalu River to their Chinese base. The sixth went into a dive pursued by an F-80. Taking advantage of his plane's slight speed advantage in a dive, the U.S. pilot narrowed the distance between himself and his prey, and with a burst of .50-caliber fire sent the MiG-15 spiraling earthward in a fatal plunge.

The world's first duel between jets, an American victory, was over in less than a minute. As the ensuing months of the Korean War would show, combat in the new jet age unrolled at quicksilver speed, with fighters racing toward each other faster than 20 miles a minute. "The old razzle-dazzle, ham-fisted fighter pilot is out," said one U.S. air force colonel. "Now it's accurate, precision, feather-touch flying."

Ultimately unequal to the heavily armed, sweptwing MiG (named for its Russian designers, Mikoyan and Gurevich), the F-80 was soon replaced by America's own sweptwing, the F-86 Sabre. Whizzing along at a record-shattering 675 mph, the Sabre had controls so responsive, in the words of one pilot, that "they seemed actuated by thought." The Sabre and the MiG were strikingly similar in performance, the MiG slightly more maneuverable, the Sabre steadier at high speeds. Later in the war, upgraded Sabres and their well-trained pilots would rack up a kill ratio of more than 17 to 1 against MiGs, but U.S. airmen remained in awe of the enemy plane. In June 1953, future man on the moon Buzz Aldrin (above, right) scored his second MiG kill after a lengthy dogfight. It was, he later recalled, "the hairiest experience I've had flying machines in this planet's atmosphere."

Future astronaut Buzz Aldrin climbs into the cockpit of his F-86 Sabre. During his first MiG kill, the jet's gun camera filmed as he was firing, recording the sequence below—the first combat images of a pilot ejecting.

Moments after his plane is hit by gunfire from Aldrin's Sabre, the MiG-15 pilot "punches out"; the second frame (top right) captures the burst of flame of the ejection seat's explosive launch.

Cold War Muscle

The U.S. Strategic Air Command (SAC) was one of the strongest military forces in history, and yet it accomplished its mission without ever firing a bullet or dropping a bomb. Born of the American desire to avoid a nuclear-age Pearl Harbor, SAC began life in March 1946 relatively ill equipped for the long-range offensive and reconnaissance operations it was formed to conduct. Two years later it found its champion: cigar-chewing brass-tacks air force lieutenant general Curtis LeMay *(below)*, architect of the strategic bombing of Japan in World War II.

Curtis LeMay

With apocalyptic fervor LeMay pursued his vision of a round-the-clock "war against war." As Cold War tensions with the Soviet Union mounted, LeMay went slashing through bureaucratic red tape to build a global web of forward bases and bring his aging bomber fleet up to jet-age snuff. In 1952 SAC began stationing its medium-range B-47 workhorse everywhere from Guam to Morocco to Maine. Three years later, the B-52 Stratofortress, with its awesome range of 6,000 miles, enabled SAC strike forces to fly directly from North American bases. Airborne refueling tankers extended that range even farther *(right)*. Refueling was a dangerous proposition: More than 600,000 pounds of aircraft had to maneuver so that tanker and bomber were only 30 feet apart while a boom delivered lifeblood to the bomber's turbojets. Every six minutes, LeMay liked to boast, at least one SAC plane was being refueled somewhere in the air.

By the mid-1950s SAC's mission was clear: to deter Soviet aggression by threatening a devastating nuclear response. Within a few short years, the single-minded air force general had bombers in the sky 24 hours a day—each plane ready to deliver as much as eight megatons of

Armed with two nuclear-tipped missiles, a B-52 nuzzles up to the fuel boom of a tanker. SAC bombers routinely flew 24-hour-long training missions, refueling several times in flight.

Closed-circuit TV cameras broadcast activities at SAC's combat control center (above) to bases around the world. Flight crews wore full gear even to church (left), prepared at any moment to rush to their planes; the crew below heads for a jet serving as the airborne command post.

bombs to its assigned targets. The system he established remained essentially unchanged for more than 30 years, until the Cold War was over.

The brain behind that system was an electronic-combat control center buried 50 feet under Offutt Air Force Base in Omaha, presumably safe from a Soviet nuclear attack. Procedures were carefully scripted and even more meticulously rehearsed. "No-notice" drills began with the simulated detection of incoming Soviet aircraft or missiles, which sent controllers at Offutt to the red phone to put SAC's entire global force on immediate alert. Six minutes later, bombers not already in the air would be roaring down their runways. Planes then proceeded to their fail-safe point, typically just outside the perimeter of Soviet airspace, beyond which a bomber could not proceed without a direct order from the president. Were that order to come, the crew could only arm their bombs with codes delivered from Offutt or from one of SAC's five airborne command posts, each a specially converted tanker jet that could manage the entire system as a backup.

The bomber crews carrying out SAC's work became a breed quite literally apart. With every team expected to take off at a moment's notice, men lived for days on end in bombproof underground bunkers and slept in rubber-and-nylon flight suits to shave precious seconds from the time it took during an alert to race to the runway. During the long flights their heads were entombed in steel-and-glass helmets, and they had to sit on their survival packs because the bombers were so crowded with controls. The stratosphere's thin air left them severely dehydrated.

The stress of all this, on top of poor pay and substandard housing, ruined many a marriage. But morale remained high. Under LeMay's command, the number of aircraft lost or damaged for every 100,000 hours of flying time plunged from 65 down to three. To SAC fliers, LeMay was the high priest of nuclear deterrence, and they were his acolytes. More than a few took up cigar chewing in homage.

A squadron of B-47 Stratojets passes over-head in formation. SAC pilots loved flying the sleek, sweptwing bomber, which some said handled just like a fighter.

With a fuselage of wafer-thin aluminum and gliderlike wings for high-altitude cruising, the U-2 was tailored for long flights 15 miles above the earth's surface.

Stratospheric Spy

Deterrence was at least in part based on knowing what the enemy was up to, but when it came to Soviet missile deployment, the U.S. had very little to go on. So in 1955 the Central Intelligence Agency assigned aircraft manufacturer Lockheed the project of building a spy plane that would be able to penetrate deep within Soviet airspace for reconnaissance, then return unharmed.

If anyone was equal to the task, it was Lockheed's legendary chief research engineer, Clarence "Kelly" Johnson. He led a group of crack engineers who had developed the prototype of America's first operational jet fighter in just 143 days back in the 1940s. Known as Skunk Works—to maintain secrecy at Lockheed, they worked out of a circus tent alongside a malodorous plastics factory—Johnson's outfit got busy designing a craft that could fly high enough and long enough to accomplish the mission. The result: the sleek U-2 *(above)*.

Gary Powers

In 1956, a short year after the blueprints were on the table, "Kelly's Angel" made its maiden voyage over the Soviet Union.

In designing the U-2, the Skunk Works team squeezed out every last foot of range and altitude, ending up with a plane that could fly deep-penetration missions a dazzling 70,000 feet above the earth, well beyond the reach of Soviet missiles and fighters. Although the United States denied its existence, the Soviets certainly knew something was up

there: They could detect it by radar. But for four years U-2s sailed over Soviet territory with impunity, their cameras clicking away while Soviet Air Defense commanders shook their fists.

Then in 1960 they got one. On May Day, CIA-employed pilot Francis Gary Powers *(left)* was approaching the airspace over the town of Sverdlovsk when suddenly there was a blinding orange flash and his U-2's fragile wings were torn off. Powers parachuted to safety but was captured. Later it would come out that the U-2 had been downed by shock waves from a battery of upgraded surface-to-air missiles.

Immediately the CIA had NASA declare that one of its weather research planes flying over Turkey had veered off course. On the eve of a U.S.-Soviet summit, Premier Nikita Khrushchev *(right)* announced that Powers had confessed, and an embarrassed Eisenhower was forced to admit the spy operation. In an international show trial orchestrated by Khrushchev, Powers was sentenced to 10 years' imprisonment. Home after a spy swap two years later, he was vilified by macho patriots for not having used the poisoned suicide needle in his flight kit. The tight-lipped U.S. government made its sleuth out to be a lone ranger on an isolated spy mission. It wasn't until 1993 that the truth began to emerge: Powers, a public pawn in the high-stakes game of Cold War chess, was just one of thousands of American airmen who had made top-secret "ferret" flights over Soviet territory. Many had never come back.

Despite this inauspicious episode, the high-flying U-2 went on to validate the effort of Johnson's Skunk Works many times over. In 1962 it was the U-2 that recorded the alarming buildup of Soviet offensive missiles in Cuba. More

Appearing before the Soviet Union's ruling body, Premier Nikita Khrushchev brandishes a photograph allegedly taken by Powers's U-2. The Soviet leader invited the pilot's parents to visit their son, noting in his telegram that Powers would be "tried according to the laws of the Soviet Union."

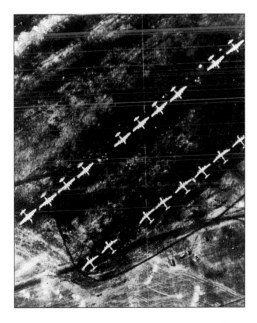

This aerial photograph was said to be from film recovered from the wreckage of the downed U-2.

The U-2's scattered pieces were purportedly gathered together to form this pile of debris. Other recovered items put on display included Powers's flight suit and helmet.

than 40 years after its debut, an upgraded version remains the number one U.S. reconnaissance plane.

Blackbird Beauty. Almost as soon as the U-2 was in the air, Skunk Works' chief designer Johnson was dreaming up its successor, a reconnaissance superplane that would fly more than 80,000 feet up at a record-shattering cruising speed of well over mach 3.

Unlike the U-2, the SR-71 Blackbird was four years in the making, and virtually everything about it had to be invented from scratch. The design included the first-ever use of radar-defeating stealth technology, but many of the most unusual features specifically addressed the fact that air friction at sustained ultrahigh speeds would heat the plane's surface to as much as 1,000 degrees Fahrenheit. One brilliant move was to add corrugations in the wing *(right)*—reminiscent of the corrugated fuselages of much older planes—to allow the metal to expand without warping; as Johnson noted, "I was accused of trying to make a 1932 Ford Tri-Motor go Mach 3, but the concept worked."

The Blackbird made its first test flight in 1962. It had two imposing high-thrust jet engines and, for stability, a fuselage flared out like the fins on a manta ray. The pilot had to wear a 40-pound pressure suit designed to prevent blackouts and give him at least a chance of surviving if forced to eject while flashing through the semidarkness at the edge of space.

For some time the existence of the Blackbird was denied, and many details about it remain murky. In 1966 it entered service with SAC, went on to record such milestones as China's first H-bomb explosion, and visited every hot spot on the globe from North Vietnam to the Persian Gulf. Its spy cameras were as outstanding as the craft itself, recording details as small as the writing on a golf ball from 85,000 feet up.

At a cost of $200,000 for a single hour of flight, and with sophisticated satellite technology coming of age, the Blackbird was retired in 1990. But it had set the stage for more Skunk Works oddities to come.

Designed for speed, the surreal Blackbird had a flared fuselage for stability and was painted black to help radiate heat from its titanium skin.

The Chopper War

O ne of the first of many lessons America learned in Vietnam was that technological superiority in the air did not always guarantee success on the ground. In the early 1960s, when American involvement in Vietnam began, most U.S. aircraft were tailored primarily for the SAC mission of taking out Soviet targets from a safe distance—not for close air support and tactical bombing against an enemy hidden under a jungle canopy. Only one flying machine in the U.S. arsenal—the helicopter—seemed made for the Vietnamese terrain, but it too would have its troubles. In Vietnam, it seemed, there was often just no way to win.

With their ability to hover and fly vertically, helicopters were able to penetrate otherwise inaccessible areas to counteract the Vietcong's hit-and-run tactics. By the mid-1960s, a typical mission involved both nimble Huey escorts and heavily laden troop transports such as the Choctaw. The Hueys would spray any cover near a landing site with machine-gun fire, then hover overhead like guardian angels while the Choctaws went whirring down to disgorge their troops. For the chopper pilots, as for the soldiers on the ground, the fear was palpable. Every pilot knew that a well-aimed burst of fire could bring his bird down; indeed, thousands of times the guardian angels turned out to be sitting ducks for snipers. Eventually, helicopters only went in after an area had been strafed and bombed by less vulnerable jets.

More than anything else, the dull thud of chopper blades came to symbolize the grim realities of Vietnam and the ambivalent feelings it stirred. Sometimes helicopters were agents of terror, storming in en masse and raking the ground with a withering fire. Sometimes they were saviors, rescuing trapped units and airlifting the wounded to safety. And sometimes they were the nation's pallbearers, bringing its sons back in body bags. For many Americans, the final, lasting image of U.S. involvement summed it up: a lone helicopter lifting off from a Saigon rooftop, still serving in a now-lost cause.

A marine at the gun mount of a CH-34 (inset) stands ready to fire at enemy positions near a landing zone where the transport helicopter is about to drop troops.

South Vietnamese soldiers scramble out of CH-34s to launch an attack against Vietcong infantry hidden behind the distant tree line; the vulnerable choppers lift away immediately.

While helicopter pilots primarily dealt with events on the ground, their jet-flying colleagues were waging war far aloft, blistering North Vietnam with one of the most intensive bombing campaigns in history. Bomber and fighter pilots faced their own challenges, particularly in the war's early stages, and they soon learned that success required outsmarting as well as outgunning the enemy.

During bombing runs, strike formations of F-105 Thunderchief fighter-bombers, escorted by F-4 Phantoms, were running afoul of a clever enemy tactic: MiGs would sneak up above the formations, single out the more vulnerable Thunderchiefs, then try to score—often with success—while diving to the safety of their airfields. The big problem was that by the time the F-4 Phantoms could react, the MiGs had fled.

The U.S. response, known as Operation Bolo, was masterminded by Colonel Robin Olds *(right),* a charismatic World War II ace who was greatly admired by his men. The plan was based on an ingenious ruse: Phantoms armed with air-to-air missiles would, in effect, fly like Thun-

derchiefs—adopting their altitude, airspeed, and call signs —in an attempt to lure the skittish MiGs into combat and then shoot them down.

On January 2, 1967, Bolo was put into action. Olds set out with almost 100 planes for the enemy air base at Phuc Yen. It was a cloudy day. They flew over the base, circled around, then got their nibble as MiG-21s began popping through the overcast. With his radarscope dot centered on a target, Olds fired off a succession of Sparrow and Sidewinder missiles, but they failed to track. Finally one Sparrow did hit home, exploding forward of the target's tail. The MiG cartwheeled, went into a flat spin, and vanished beneath the clouds. By the end of Operation Bolo a total of seven MiGs had been bagged. It was a stunning success.

But the success didn't last. For one thing, the Phantoms were not designed for short-range encounters. For another, the men who flew them were woefully deficient in the old-fashioned art of dogfighting. So in 1969 the U.S. Navy set about reviving that art, establishing a school that would come to be known as Top Gun. (The air force would have its own version, named Red Flag.) There pilots flew in mock combat against older U.S. aircraft that were comparable in performance

Colonel Robin Olds is borne aloft by his pilots after completing 100 combat missions over North Vietnam.

An F-4 Phantom fires rockets at entrenched enemy positions in a South Vietnamese hamlet. To
minimize the chance of being shot down, strafing
jets typically zoomed in on targets at 500 mph.

Lieutenants Randy Cunningham (right) and Willie Driscoll be-came the Vietnam War's first U.S. aces on May 10, 1972. Stars on their F-4's intake display their squadron's cumulative MiG kills.

Fighters and strike aircraft crowd the flight deck of the USS Con-stellation prior to Cunningham and Driscoll's record-setting sortie. They had to eject from their F-4 on the way back.

to MiGs. In the skies over Miramar Naval Air Station in San Diego, students learned and then polished a battery of sophisticated maneuvers that would have amazed the likes of von Richthofen and Rickenbacker.

As late as 1972, the U.S. still did not have a single ace in Vietnam; even Olds was one short of the requisite five kills. But that would change soon after Randy "Duke" Cun-ningham came out of Top Gun. An F-4 pilot aboard the USS carrier *Constellation*, Lieutenant Cunningham was just as bright, brash, and cocksure as any of Top Gun's elite fighter jocks. He and his radar intercept officer, Lieutenant Willie Driscoll, had taken out two MiGs in the space of five months when, on May 10, 1972, they brought down three

"As I looked back over my ejection seat I got the surprise of my life: There was the MiG, canopy to canopy with me, barely 300 feet away!"

Randy "Duke" Cunningham

more in a single, nerve-racking mission that would catapult them into the coveted galaxy of America's wartime aces.

On that day their Phantom shot off the *Constellation*'s flight deck as part of a bombing strike force. Soon after the bombing began, Cunningham and Driscoll got a call from their wingman: Two MiG-17s were boring in on their tail, the lead one's nose spitting tracer fire. Cunningham knew from his Top Gun training that the MiG-17 couldn't change course quickly at high speed, so he broke hard, and the on-coming plane overshot. Now on his enemy's tail, he squeezed off a heat-seeking Sidewinder and watched as it hit home.

Seconds later another Phantom flashed by with a num-ber of MiGs in pursuit. Cunningham rolled in behind. "Break right!" he radioed the Phantom pilot. By now there were MiGs everywhere, four on Cunningham's own tail and several more above. When the other Phantom was clear of his target path, Cunningham called "Fox Two!"—the radio signal for firing a Sidewinder—and squeezed the trigger. The missile ripped through one of the MiGs and blew it to bits.

By now Cunningham and Driscoll had lost track of their wingman and decided to head back. Suddenly another MiG-17 appeared out of nowhere, coming straight at them. Cunningham tried to skate past the plane at close range; that way, he knew from Top Gun, it couldn't turn and latch onto his tail. But as the distance narrowed, Cunningham recalled, "the MiG's entire nose lit up like a Christmas tree. Pumpkin-sized BBs went sailing by our F-4." Without guns to reciprocate, Cunningham pulled straight up and assumed the MiG would head home. To his surprise, the enemy aircraft nosed right up behind him, so close the two planes were barely 300 feet apart, and engaged Cunningham in a deadly dogfight involving a series of intricate vertical maneuvers not typical of MiG pilots *(box, right)*.

Finally Cunningham made a last-ditch effort to break the pas de deux: On a vertical zoom he popped his speed brakes, yanked his throttles to idle, and watched the MiG shoot ahead of him. Over the top they went again, but this time the U.S. pilot was on his enemy's tail. As the two planes headed straight down, he let loose a Sidewinder, thought it had missed, and was about to fire another when the MiG burst into flame. It flew straight into the ground.

Still more trouble was waiting. As they headed back toward their ship, a surface-to-air missile exploded near them and crippled the F-4's hydraulic system. Cunningham's only way to steer was with the rudder. For 20 miles the Phantom yawed violently as they struggled to reach the safety of open water. Just as they crossed the coastline, an explosion ripped through the Phantom, which stalled and went into a spin. They ejected and 15 minutes later were picked up by marine helicopters.

The *Constellation* gave the returning heroes a rousing reception. Arriving on the flight deck, Cunningham was handed a shirt that read, "General Robin Olds 4, Duke 5."

The Mysterious Colonel Tomb

The superb MiG-17 pilot who drew Randy Cunningham into an intricate dogfight and died as a result (see text at left) was said to be the legendary Colonel Tomb. Credited with 13 kills, Tomb was a ghostly presence; he may or may not be the North Vietnamese pilot in the photograph above, apparently instructing students on dogfighting with a pair of models. Indeed, he may not have existed at all: The fact that the North Vietnamese never publicized any of his baker's dozen kills led U.S. airmen to surmise that Tomb was a composite of several pilots—perhaps Chinese and Soviet fliers whose identities, for reasons of diplomacy, had to be kept quiet.

Whoever his adversary, Cunningham was understandably taken off guard by the skills he displayed. Few North Vietnamese pilots had been known to even engage Phantoms, and fewer still had taken part in the sort of vertical dogfight that ensued. Their canned "shoot-and-scoot" tactics reflected their regimented training. Unlike the American pilots, who learned classic maneuvers at Top Gun and then were expected to think for themselves in combat, these Communist airmen flew in the tight grip of ground control. Thus, despite the subsonic MiG-17's ability to turn on a dime and the supersonic MiG-21's impressive performance at high altitudes, North Vietnamese aviators hardly ever performed maneuvers more complex than level turning pursuits. The pilot who dueled with Cunningham on May 10, 1972, may very well have been disobeying an order to return to base. Perhaps, after all, there was a one-of-a-kind "Colonel Tomb" up there that day.

Gulf War Mastery

Technology proved itself as never before over the deserts of Iraq and Kuwait in 1991. In the years following Vietnam, designers toiled to produce planes that were more maneuverable and could respond more intelligently to the conditions of combat. By the time of the Gulf War, 1970s- and 1980s-vintage aircraft had evolved into modern-day platforms for waging electronic warfare and planting munitions with surgical precision.

These upgraded conventional craft were only a portion of the huge air armada in Desert Storm, the war to oust Saddam Hussein from Kuwait. More than 2,000 aircraft from 32 nations took part. Coordinating their activity around the clock made commercial air traffic control look like kindergarten. The daily script was 600 pages long; known as the Air Tasking Order (ATO), it assigned flight paths and roles for each plane, even specifying minute details such as the moment individual bombs should detonate.

On top of it all, the whole massive effort had to be made intelligible to the public that bankrolled it. CNN beamed the reassuring face of the operation's commander, U.S. Army general Norman Schwarzkopf (inset), into American dens so that he could recount Desert Storm's progress. Part teacher, part cheerleader, Schwarzkopf wowed his audience with the high-tech muscle of coalition forces—especially U.S. air power.

Months of close planning went into the opening gambit alone. In the predawn hours of January 17, 1991, four huge AWACS planes took up position south of the Iraqi border, their 30-foot rotating radar domes probing the darkness for enemy aircraft. Soon KC-135 airborne tankers began topping off combat aircraft as they roared aloft from their airfields and carriers, radios silent, waiting word to cross into Iraqi airspace. This first wave of almost 100 planes consisted primarily of conventional aircraft crammed with the latest gear. Adaptations of existing designs led to a veritable alphabet soup of names, among them F-15C Eagle fighters to pick off any interceptors, EF-111 Ravens to jam radar, F-4G Wild Weasels to launch radar-homing missiles, and F-111F Aardvarks and A-6E Intruders to deliver bombs.

But there were two completely novel raiders as well, and at this very

A navy F-14 Tomcat cruises over Kuwait's burning oil fields. During Desert Storm, F-14s took part in special reconnaissance missions and flew cover for ships in the Red Sea and Persian Gulf.

Lieutenant Colonel Rick Rife, standing by an Apache, took part in several Desert Storm missions. "The training was harder than the actual combat," he noted afterward.

"There was a lot of pressure on this mission. If we didn't do 100 percent, . . . a lot of people were going to get hurt."

Chief Warrant Officer Lou Hall

The Apache's Target Acquisition Designation Sight brought war to a video screen. Here the pilot has an M88 tank fixed in his cross hairs.

moment they were slipping past Iraqi defenses on their way to Baghdad ahead of all the others. Sea-launched Tomahawks—winged, auto-guided jet missiles that bore an eerie resemblance to aircraft—skimmed the ground below radar's reach; and the ace up the U.S. Air Force's sleeve, 15 F-117A stealth fighters, stole in like wraiths, invisible to radar detection.

Before the conventional armada of strike planes could be dispatched, a pair of early-warning radar installations near Iraq's southern border would have to be blinded. That job had been given to eight Apache AH-64 helicopters *(right)*. The Apache was a roving, armor-plated arsenal of doom, the U.S. Army's answer to the post-Vietnam need for attack helicopters. In addition to a mounted 30-mm chain gun, it could tote both 2.75-inch rockets and laser-guided Hellfire missiles. Shortly before 2 a.m., eight Apaches escorted by the air force's Pave Low electronic-warfare choppers sneaked across the border in two separate teams, lights off and in complete radio silence.

The pilots flew only 50 feet above the ground with the aid of night-vision goggles, forward-looking infrared radar (FLIR) screens, and the Pave Low's terrain-following radar. Within nine miles of the targets, the Pave Lows used their Global Positioning Systems to fix release points for the Apaches' Hellfires, dropping chemical light on the desert floor. Then the two Apache teams shot invisible laser beams on the radar installations and closed in.

Everything was moving with clockwork precision. The Hellfires had been timed to fire at exactly 2:38. On cue, the radio silence was broken: "Party in 10!" came the fire command from the lead team. "Joy in 10!" answered the other team. Ten seconds later a salvo of Hellfires knifed along their laser paths straight into the heart of their targets. Videotape systems recorded the results. One warrant officer noted that watching white bursts on tiny black-and-green screens was "exactly like a video game. You just shoot, you don't really see the guys getting torn up." The reality was anything but a game. Buildings and vehicles crumbled under the sudden hail of missiles, 30-mm bullets, and rockets scattering a deadly confetti of razor-sharp projectiles called flechettes. Thirty seconds later both sites were disabled. Four minutes into the action the radar bases had been obliterated.

The Apaches, in Schwarzkopf's words, had "plucked out the eyes" of Iraq's air defenses. With a radar-black corridor into Iraq now open, the first wave of nonstealthy aircraft slipped through unseen.

Meanwhile, the Tomahawk cruise missiles and the F-117 stealth

Equipped with armored seats and protective plating, AH-64 Apaches were sturdy tank busters that could take punishment as well as dole it out. During the January 17, 1991, raid, they were fired at with small arms but came through unscathed.

Barely visible even with night-vision imaging, an F-117 stealth fighter inches toward a tanker's refueling boom over Saudi Arabia in January 1991.

fighters were bearing down on Baghdad. The Tomahawks arrived first. No sooner had they struck than the city, home to one of the densest air defense networks on earth, began tossing up antiaircraft fire so thick that in the eyes of approaching stealth pilots individual tracers fused into an orange, charcoal-like glow. But Baghdad's response was a confused, spasmodic flailing. The F-117s slipped between the cracks. They came not in traditional formation, replete with escorts, but singly—black against the night sky, cruising over the ancient city like shadowy Batmobiles.

The startling new planes that were about to plant their laser-guided smart bombs in Saddam Hussein's nerve center were yet another product of Lockheed's supersecretive Skunk Works (page 142). Continuing its reputation for no-nonsense, top-quality work, the Skunk Works had designed and built the stealth fighter in just 31 months—on schedule and under budget. The result was an ingenious flying machine. Though its wingspan stretched more than 40 feet, the F-117 reflected no more radar energy than a hummingbird. Flat, sharply angled surfaces sent radar scattering. A fiber-and-resin paint absorbed any leftover beams. Engines were buried deep within the plane, their roar muted and their hot parts concealed from heat-seeking missiles.

These ghostly wonder planes materialized over Baghdad at around three o'clock, the only aircraft that would be allowed to venture within its lethal airspace during the entire war. In their cockpits sat air force pilots expert in the art of night bombing. Some came playing rock and roll. Some prayed. To avoid being distracted by snaking tracers and popcorn puffs of heavy artillery, some flew in with their eyes fixed on their instrument panels.

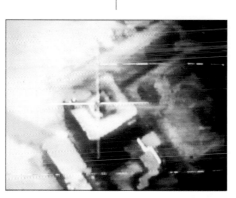

Each plane carried two 14-foot-long, 2,000-pound laser-guided bombs.

One site slated for destruction was Iraqi air force headquarters in downtown Baghdad. The building, picked up by an infrared sensor, slid into view on the pilot's television-like screen. Fixing his laser beam on a ventilation shaft in the roof, he waited for a signal from the fire-control computer to release his bomb. With exact timing, the hotdog-shaped weapon went sailing down its laser path, plunged through the shaft, and blew the headquarters apart. The other F-117s went about their job with equally uncanny precision, launching bombs that sliced into underground command bunkers, communications hubs, power plants, and numerous other sites. That night over Baghdad and elsewhere in Iraq and Kuwait, stealth fighters took out roughly one-third of the ATO's listed targets without receiving a scratch.

During the next few weeks conventional aircraft performed admirably too, not least because Saddam was keeping his MiGs on the ground, presumably saving them for another day. Among the standouts were A-10 Warthogs, which proved their worth taking out trucks that carried Scud missiles, and agile F-16s that flew more than 13,000 sorties against everything from airfields to weapons factories. So effective was the combined air muscle that when on February 24 Schwarzkopf's coalition army went into action against Saddam's Republican Guard in Kuwait, the ground war lasted a mere 100 hours.

The technologies that had been maturing for the previous two decades—stealth, precision guidance, and integrated electronics—had come together in history's first remote-control war. By keeping ground troops from becoming mired in battle, air power had fulfilled its potential.

The image above shows the video screen view of a stealth fighter's targeting: Using cross hairs, the pilot fixes a laser beam on his target and waits for a fire-control signal telling him when to "pickle off" his bomb. In Baghdad, buildings next to targeted structures were left largely untouched.

Like something straight out of science fiction, a
B-2 bomber—the stealth fighter's big brother—
slices through the sky on a practice run.

Advantage: Stealth

I t has a wingspan more than half the length of a football field but is invisible to radar. It can carry all types of bombs—"dumb" or smart, conventional or nuclear—and tote them almost halfway around the world. Known as the Spirit, the B-2 stealth bomber is a marvel of aviation technology and a fitting symbol of the new millennium in flight.

This saw-toothed boomerang had old roots. Back in 1923, aircraft designer Jack Northrop dreamed of a pure "flying wing" with no tail or fuselage to create drag. But such a craft would be inherently unstable, so it wasn't until the 1970s that the concept became feasible with the advent of fly-by wire flight control.

The two-billion-dollar plane made its combat debut on March 24, 1999, when a pair of Spirits took off from Whiteman Air Force Base in Missouri, flew to Yugoslavia to dislodge 16 one-ton bombs each, then turned back home. For the pilots, the Spirit was a dream to fly. And with its stealth features crews were confident about being out of harm's way. During the 30-hour round trip one pilot could nap, read, or heat up chili dogs while the other bent over computer displays. These fliers were farther removed from the field of battle than at any time in history, and after a mission they slept between their own sheets. "My pilots come home every day," one B-2 captain said. "You can't put a dollar on that."

Beyond the Sky

★

FLYING INTO SPACE

As their flimsy biplane sputtered to life on the beach at Kitty Hawk, Wilbur and Orville had no idea of the thunder that would roar just a few hundred miles to their south in the years to come. Orville lived to see some of the wondrous offspring their invention would foster, but when he died in 1948, the century's last great aeronautical leap still lay in the future, the stuff of dreams.

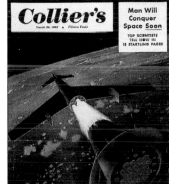

In 1952, *Collier's* magazine ran a series of articles on those dreams. The series featured several forward-thinking scientists, including a renowned German rocket engineer named Wernher von Braun, and the cover of the first issue (*inset*) featured one of his designs: a multistage winged spaceship. Von Braun envisioned such vehicles shuttling people and supplies to orbiting space stations from which interplanetary explorations would be launched.

Skeptics dismissed von Braun's theories, but before the close of the decade, one of his rockets would lift an American satellite into orbit. Ten years later, another would carry the first men to the moon. And thirty years after the *Collier's* series, America's space program would focus its energies on operating a manned shuttle that very much resembled von Braun's. Flying had come a long way from Kitty Hawk.

The shuttle Atlantis, winged for reentry like von Braun's 1952 design (above), blasts off for space in 1988. Its three main engines and attached boosters generate some 6.5 million pounds of thrust.

Off with a Blast

A German V-2 rocket designed by Wernher von Braun awaits liftoff (above). Named the Vengeance Weapon by Hitler, this missile traveled at five times the speed of sound, reached 50 miles up on its trajectory, and hit targets almost 200 miles away.

A youthful von Braun—member in good standing of the German Society for Space Travel, a group of engineers experimenting with rocket design—shoulders a model around 1930.

The idea was as old as Chinese fireworks, but rocketry didn't come into its own until the 20th century. The secret was the discovery, by American Robert Goddard, among others *(opposite)*, that liquid propellants packed a much bigger wallop than the traditional solid fuel, gunpowder. Soon Goddard was blasting missiles more than a mile and a half high. At first his colleagues saw little practical use for these long-range projectiles, but soon enough they were jolted into an alarming recognition of their worth.

In 1944, Adolf Hitler's forces began launching armed missiles at targets nearly 200 miles away in France, Belgium, and England. They were the latest generation of Wernher von Braun's liquid-fueled Aggregat rocket, the V-2 *(above, left)*. The 20-year-old von Braun had joined the German army's rocket program in 1932 in the hope that it would further his boyhood dream of building a craft that could reach space. His first model, the Aggregat-1, took "exactly one-half year to build," he later recalled, "and one-half second to blow up." But by 1934 von Braun had built a second version, fueled by a mixture of liquid oxygen and alcohol, that climbed more than a mile high. A few years later Hitler authorized the large-scale production of an even better version, which with customary menace the Fuhrer dubbed the Vengeance Weapon.

Aimed primarily at London, the V-2 did induce terror: Because it traveled faster than sound, it struck its victims before they heard it coming, crashing out of the sky without warning. But with only a rudimentary guidance system, many V-2s wildly missed their marks. In any event, the die was already cast in

Europe, and the world's first ballistic missile proved largely meaningless.

As Germany fell, its top brains headed both east and west. Von Braun and his colleagues ended up with the Allies, and before long they were sharing their accomplishments with American scientists at army bases in the United States.

Quite naturally, von Braun assumed that America—home of the great Robert Goddard—would be far along in rocketry, and he was eager to help the United States find a way to send men into space as early as 1950. Much to his surprise, however, not only did America have no space program, but Goddard's ideas about space travel had been virtually ignored. Von Braun's assignment was to be purely military: to launch salvaged V-2s and to develop better ballistic missiles for the army.

Decision makers in the United States knew full well that the Soviet Union had reaped its share of German rocket talent, and as the Cold War began, rocket warfare loomed as an undeniable threat. The goal, therefore, was to design missiles whose range would be not merely national but intercontinental, and to use rockets to send artificial satellites into orbit; such satellites would carry instruments to study atmospheric conditions and other phenomena, but equipped with the best spy cameras, they could also act as reconnaissance craft to penetrate the veil of secrecy surrounding the Soviet Union.

In the early 1950s von Braun's army team had a rocket, called Jupiter C, that the German scientist said could propel a satellite into orbit. But President Eisenhower chose instead to go with the navy's Vanguard project, which was still on the drawing board. He did so in part because Vanguard had no military history and could be presented to the public as a program developed for peaceable purposes. And since White House experts were confident that American technology was still far superior to that of the Soviets, Eisenhower believed there was plenty of time to develop a brand-new product.

As work proceeded on the missile program, experi-

Robert Goddard

Hermann Oberth

Konstantin Tsiolkovsky

First Rocketeers

Three scientists in three different countries came to the same conclusion in the early 1900s: Liquid-fueled rockets could take humans into space. In 1903, Russian inventor Konstantin Tsiolkovsky hypothesized that a rocket burning propellants such as liquid oxygen and liquid hydrogen would have enough power to break free of earth's gravity. German theorist Hermann Oberth, in his 1923 publication "The Rocket into Interplanetary Space," argued that such machines would be able to fly to the moon and other planets and could even carry people, "probably without endangering their health." Oberth's book inspired a generation of German rocket engineers, including Wernher von Braun. But Robert Goddard, an American physicist and inventor, justly laid claim to being the father of modern rocketry. On March 16, 1926, in Auburn, Massachusetts, he put his own and his fellow rocket men's theories successfully to the test, launching the first ever liquid-fueled rocket (above).

Test pilot Neil Armstrong, wearing a special life-support flight suit, stands next to an X-15. In 1962 he flew the rocket-powered craft to 207,500 feet—only 11 miles short of the boundary of space.

Still securely attached under the wing of its B-52 mother ship, an X-15 waits to be drop-launched (above). After release (inset), less than 90 seconds of engine burn would propel it to speed and altitude records for aircraft that have never been matched.

ments with rocket-powered aircraft continued. Building on the technology that had produced the supersonic X-1 *(pages 122-126)*, a group from the air force, the navy, and the National Advisory Committee for Aeronautics (NACA) began designing a "hypersonic" plane—one that could fly at least five times the speed of sound. The exciting possibility was that such a plane might be able to exit the earth's atmosphere and fly right into space.

In 1954, their efforts started bearing fruit with the creation of the X-15, a dartlike, snub-winged craft designed to break mach 6—literally twice as fast as a speeding bullet—and reach altitudes beyond 50 miles, climbing right to the edge of space. Because of its extraordinary speed, range officers set aside an exceptionally large area for testing. A special flight corridor known as the High Range was reserved for the X-15 along a series of dry lake

beds stretching 485 miles northeast from Edwards Air Force Base, the former Muroc *(pages 122-123)*.

Designing such a machine posed a host of challenges, many centered on keeping the plane intact and ensuring the pilot's safety; for one thing, he had to be fully suited to survive the extreme conditions. But one of the most intriguing problems involved control. When the X-15 ventured close to the limits of the earth's atmosphere, it would lose its normal aerodynamics in the thin air; in effect, there would be no atmosphere to steer through. The solution was a control system composed of small rockets placed in the plane's nose and wings that, when fired, would alter its direction in the same way that control surfaces such as ailerons usually did. These retro-rockets would turn out to be the X-15's greatest contribution to the future of spaceflight, becoming an essential feature of every maneuverable space vehicle ever built.

Veteran test pilot Scott Crossfield *(page 126)* was the first to fly the X-15, which like its predecessors was launched in midair. Between its debut in 1959 and 1968, 12 pilots—including future astronaut Neil Armstrong *(page 164)*—made a total of 199 flights in three different X-15s. NACA pilot Joe Walker experienced weightlessness for three minutes when he reached an altitude of 67 miles, and five of the pioneers were awarded special wings for passing the 50-mile mark. For a while, they were considered America's first astronauts.

The air force was also busy at work on another type of plane intended to actually go into orbit, something the X-15 could not do. The X-20, a "dynamic soaring" vehicle nicknamed the Dyna-Soar, was a winged aircraft that would blast into space, orbit the earth, then glide back home. It was a promising idea, but it never got past the design stage. Global politics had intervened.

On October 4, 1957, the Soviet Union shocked the world by launching the first artificial satellite, Sputnik. The nearly 200-pound gadget, which circled the globe every 96 minutes, emitted an eerie radio signal that could be picked up on any shortwave set. Standing in their own backyards, Americans could even see the satellite as a fast-moving speck of light in the night sky above them. News broadcasts that played its nerve-jangling "beep-beep" drilled into the minds of more than a few that the Communists were gaining in strength with every passing day. And the Soviets' intense secrecy only added to the

Its nose cone about to topple, the navy's Vanguard rocket crashes back to earth after barely lifting off the launch pad. The missile's payload, a Sputnik-like satellite (right) housed in the nose cone, ended up in nearby bushes.

Celebrating its successful launch, William Pickering, James van Allen, and Wernher von Braun of the army's satellite team hoist a replica of the first American satellite, Explorer 1. The 31-pound, four-foot Explorer flew slightly higher than anticipated, and its instruments detected a region of radiation later named the Van Allen belts.

"We have firmly established our foothold in space. We will never give it up again."

Wernher von Braun

Vanguard I satellite

worry. No one knew what they were really up to behind the Iron Curtain.

Less than a month later, the Soviets launched another satellite, Sputnik II, which was nearly five times heavier than the first and carried a living creature—a dog named Laika. It was frighteningly obvious now: The Reds were preparing to send a man into space.

Desperate to catch up, America planned a December launch for the Vanguard satellite. Press coverage of the event was huge, with CBS newsman Harry Reasoner broadcasting live from Cape Canaveral in Florida. As the countdown climaxed, a mystified Reasoner told the nation that the rocket had left the launch pad so quickly he didn't even see it go up. He had lifted his eyes too soon: After rising only a few inches, Vanguard had crashed to the ground in a fiery heap. Its satellite *(below, left)* rolled into some nearby bushes and began dutifully emitting its radio signal—such a pathetic sound that one reporter pleaded, "Why doesn't someone go out there, find it, and kill it?"

After the Vanguard debacle, President Eisenhower gave the army the go-ahead to launch a satellite atop its Jupiter C rocket, which was renamed Juno so as not to press the point that this rocket could have put an American satellite into orbit fully a year sooner than Sputnik. Less than two months later, Juno hefted the first U.S. satellite, Explorer I, into orbit, much to the delight of von Braun and his team— and the relief of U.S. officials. America was finally out of the starting blocks, and the space race was officially under way.

"Have you come from outer space?"

Woman to Yuri Gagarin, after he landed in her field

On April 12, 1961, Russian cosmonaut Yuri Gagarin (above) became the first man in space. His capsule (left), which was charred during reentry into earth's atmosphere, blew its hatch at an altitude of more than four miles; Gagarin had to eject and descend by parachute, landing in a potato field.

The Race Heats Up

To compete with the Soviets in a space race, America clearly needed a program devoted solely to that purpose. President Eisenhower also felt strongly that such an organization should be nonmilitary. So on October 1, 1958, Congress authorized the creation of the National Aeronautics and Space Administration (NASA), which absorbed the space-related activities previously conducted by the armed forces and NACA. Barely one week later, Project Mercury, America's first attempt at manned spaceflight, had begun.

NASA engineer Maxime Faget determined early on that a bell-shaped capsule was the best design for the craft that would carry an astronaut into space. It would launch narrow end up at the top of the rocket and, after separating from the launch stages, descend to earth blunt end first. Strong shielding would protect it from the heat of reentry, and the aerodynamics of the bell shape would help stabilize its descent and keep it from tumbling about. It would float down the last 21,000 feet by parachute, then deploy an air bag to cushion its ocean landing.

But who would be lodged inside? After weeks of physical and psychological tests, NASA chose seven men from a pool of 508 candidates. Those selected were all military pilots who had logged more than 1,500 hours of flight time, and by coincidence, all seven were firstborns. Among the requirements they had to meet was a size limitation: To fit into the cramped capsule, an astronaut could not be any taller than five feet, 11 inches and could weigh no more than 180 pounds. As Wally Schirra, one of those chosen, later noted, "You don't get into the Mercury spacecraft, you put it on." On April 9, 1959, NASA introduced the Mercury Seven to the public at a news conference. Caught up in the spirit of the whole adventure, *Time* magazine pronounced them "cut of the same stone as Columbus, Magellan, Daniel Boone, Orville and Wilbur Wright."

The next question, of course, was which one would be the first into space. In fact, it was none of them. Soviet cosmonaut Yuri Gagarin *(left)* earned that distinction when he made a single orbit of the earth on April 12, 1961, in his Vostok 1 capsule. Only a few weeks later, Alan Shepard rode a Redstone rocket from Cape Canaveral into a suborbital hop that lasted 15 minutes, and the nation listened rapt as America's

Astrochimp

Before the first American astronaut set foot in a Mercury capsule, NASA selected a chimpanzee named Ham (above) to test the effects of space-flight and weightlessness on a living creature. Ham mastered a routine that required him to push buttons and manipulate levers in response to flashing lights and colors; his trainers used a supposedly foolproof method in which correct responses sent a banana pellet treat into his mouth, and incorrect ones caused a small electrical jolt to his foot. Unfortunately, when Ham went up, his capsule flew faster and higher than intended, not only subjecting him to extreme gravitational forces but also causing the test equipment to fail. As a camera inside the capsule recorded, Ham banged correctly on the buttons, only to get zapped on every try. After splashdown the capsule began filling with water, nearly drowning the chimp before the recovery helicopters arrived. NASA had staged a welcoming ceremony for Ham, but by then he was tired of being cooperative. When released from the capsule, he tried to bite anything and everything that came within reach. Despite Ham's unpleasant experience, his 18-minute flight proved to American space engineers that, with a few more bugs ironed out, Mercury would work.

first man in space announced, "What a beautiful view." Shepard experimented with piloting his capsule by firing its small rocket thrusters, then splashed down safely in the Atlantic Ocean.

Encouraged by this first success, NASA followed with a second suborbital flight about 10 weeks later, piloted by Gus Grissom. After splashdown, explosive bolts on the hatch mysteriously blew, and the capsule sank just after Grissom was rescued by helicopter. Everything else had gone well, though, and American confidence was building.

An American Hero. Shepard's and Grissom's triumphs notwithstanding, the real goal was to get into orbit, and for this mission NASA turned to the most experienced member of the Mercury team. As a marine fighter pilot during two wars, 40-year-old John Glenn *(page 172)* had forged the reputation of being able to handle planes so combat damaged that other pilots considered them unflyable. His ability to manage the unexpected counted as much as anything in NASA's choice.

The rocket that would hurl Glenn into space was a new design, called Atlas, that had been developed by the air force as an intercontinental-range missile. Never intended to support the weight of a space capsule, the Atlas initially proved wanting, exploding twice during tests with an unmanned Mercury capsule mounted atop. After a series of time-consuming modifications, the model was finally deemed ready. On February 20, 1962, with Glenn safely strapped in, *Friendship 7* climbed skyward as the mighty Atlas scorched the launch pad. From ground control, fellow astronaut Scott Carpenter radioed a simple message: "Godspeed, John Glenn." It was a moment America would never forget.

On May 5, 1961, Alan Shepard steps off a transfer van and heads toward the gantry elevator that will lift him to the top of the Redstone rocket. Because of bad weather and a computer glitch, Shepard had to wait more than four hours in the Freedom 7 capsule before blasting off on his 15-minute flight.

Wearing their spacesuits of rubber and aluminized nylon, the Mercury Seven astronauts stand for an official photograph. In the front row, left to right, are Walter "Wally" Schirra, Donald "Deke" Slayton, John Glenn, and Scott Carpenter; in the back row are Alan Shepard, Virgil "Gus" Grissom, and Gordon Cooper.

"I believe that this nation should commit itself to achieving the goal, before this decade is out, of landing a man on the moon and returning him safely to the earth."

President John F. Kennedy, May 25, 1961

Peering through the window of *Friendship*'s tiny, instrument-packed cabin, Glenn narrated his voyage to millions of listeners, describing the brilliant colors of his home planet, the flat appearance of the sun at sunset, the intensity of the stars, and the feeling of weightlessness— "something you could get addicted to," he admitted. Sailing over Australia at night he saw a large, shimmering gleam on the continent's west coast: Residents of Perth had cranked up the lights to salute Glenn as he passed over.

Later, as Glenn watched the sun come up over the curve of the earth, he saw outside his window thousands of what looked like snowflakes illuminated by the rising sun. The specks soon disappeared, only to reappear with each of the several "sunrises" he witnessed. The phenomenon remained a mystery until later flights determined that the so-called Glenn effect was a shower of ice crys-

tals dislodged from the capsule's hull as the sun heated its surface.

Glenn was nearing reentry when NASA controllers received a warning signal that *Friendship*'s heat shield had loosened. They advised Glenn not to jettison the spent retrorocket strapped to the capsule, hoping its weight would stabilize the shield. As the fiery reentry began, Glenn heard cracking noises and saw flaming chunks of metal fly past his window. But the shield held, and Glenn landed safely in the ocean. He returned to unbounded accolades from across the nation, a brand-new American hero.

"I don't know what you can say about a day in which you have seen four beautiful sunsets."

John Glenn, February 20, 1962

Thousands of New Yorkers pause to watch John Glenn's historic launch into orbit on a huge television screen in Grand Central Station. Schools brought TV sets into classrooms, and the entire nation held its breath as the countdown reached zero.

The Atlas rocket carrying John Glenn's bell-shaped capsule lifts from the launch pad on February 20, 1962. Glenn's pulse rate rose only modestly during blastoff, compared with those of Shepard and Grissom before him.

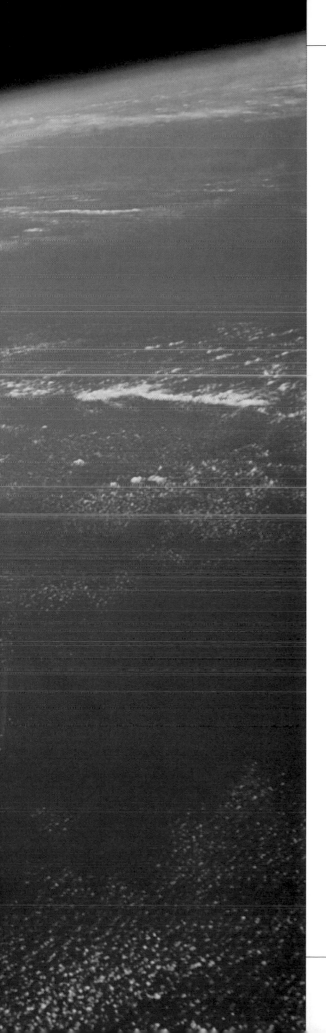

To the Moon

The goal set by President Kennedy in the heady days after Shepard's flight—a man on the moon by the end of the decade—was daunting, and after the Mercury program ran its course, much hard work still lay ahead. For the long journey to the moon, astronauts would have to learn how to maneuver a capsule precisely and to live in space for days on end. For these experiments NASA initiated a second manned project, named Gemini after the constellation of stars also known as the Twins: For each flight, two astronauts would be carried aloft. Once again, a converted intercontinental ballistic missile—this time the Titan—would provide launch power.

On June 3, 1965, Gemini 4 astronaut Edward White became the first American to "walk" in space *(inset, right)*, spending 21 minutes outside his capsule secured to it by a 25-foot "umbilical cord." White, who maneuvered by firing a hand-held gas gun or pulling on the lifeline, had so much fun that when his buddy James McDivitt beckoned him inside he grumbled, "It's the saddest moment of my life." But White's weightless jaunt put to rest NASA's fear that space-walking astronauts would suffer from vertigo or become disoriented in the empty vastness.

As it met with success after success, the Gemini project confirmed that humans could safely live in space for at least two weeks, long enough to go to the moon and back. Its astronauts deftly docked one vessel with another in orbit *(left)*, traveled 850 miles out into space—farther than ever before—and performed all manner of tasks that helped lay the groundwork for lunar missions. Indeed, by 1966, at the height of Gemini, plans were already being moved ahead for the next and final phase: Apollo.

Apollo couldn't have had a more tragic beginning. Only days before the first mission, crew member Gus Grissom told a reporter, "If we die, we

As seen from a window hatch in Gemini 6, Gemini 7 sails high above the earth (left). During orbit, the astronauts maneuvered the two craft to within a foot of each other, then flew side by side for hours practicing rendezvous techniques. This and subsequent flights helped prepare for moon missions that would involve the separation and docking of a command module and lunar lander.

"In the beginning God created the heaven and the earth. And the earth was without form . . . and darkness was on the face of the deep. . . . And God said let there be light."

William Anders of Apollo 8 reading from the Bible

The stunning beauty of the earth stands out against the rugged barrenness of the moon in this breathtaking shot from Apollo 8, taken on Christmas Eve, 1968. Crew member Jim Lovell tried to imagine whether a visitor from another planet would be able to tell that this blue green world was inhabited.

want people to accept it. We're in a risky business." Then, on January 27, 1967, as part of a series of prelaunch tests, Grissom, Ed White, and Roger Chaffee were sealed inside the cone-shaped capsule for five hours. Suddenly, a flash fire erupted and engulfed the cabin. Because of recent modifications the capsule had no quick-release hatch, and the men were trapped. All three died of asphyxiation.

It was the first major disaster for the U.S. space program and led to an extensive investigation. Studies revealed that the fire was most likely caused by an electrical short, which had ignited the capsule's volatile pure-oxygen atmosphere. Analysts accused NASA officials of taking dangerous shortcuts in their haste to beat the Soviets; in response, NASA overhauled the entire Apollo program—including its ambitious timetable.

By the close of 1968, the nation was in turmoil over Vietnam, two assassinations, and the Chicago riots, but after several missions Apollo was back on track. Apollo 8, with three astronauts aboard, thundered into space above the most powerful rocket ever built, the Saturn V. Designed by von Braun, Saturn was 36 stories tall and produced a gargantuan 7.5 million pounds of thrust at launch. Its three stages blasted the capsule out of earth's atmosphere and then lobbed it straight toward the moon.

En route, astronauts Frank Borman, James Lovell, and William Anders transmitted pictures of the earth—

the first ever of the whole planet hanging in space—to television viewers back home. While TV screens showed only black-and-white images, the astronauts breathlessly described the earth's vivid blue oceans, brilliant white clouds, and brown landscapes—a "grand oasis in the big vastness of space," said Lovell.

From lunar orbit the Apollo 8 crew sent Christmas greetings to the world, reciting the story of the Creation from the Bible. When their capsule went out of contact behind the moon's dark side, NASA controllers in Houston waited anxiously until Jim Lovell's "official" report came in loud and clear: "Please be informed there is a Santa Claus." The crew snapped hundreds of photographs of the moon's surface, including some of potential landing sites, but the most extraordinary image of all was a majestic earthrise over the stark lunar horizon *(pages 176-177)*. Earth somehow seemed more precious afterward, its troubles seen from a new perspective.

The stage was now set, and on July 20, 1969, Apollo 11 astronauts Neil Armstrong, Edwin "Buzz" Aldrin, and Michael Collins entered lunar orbit like their predecessors. This time, while Collins remained in the command module *Columbia,* Armstrong and Aldrin donned spacesuits and climbed into the spidery-looking *Eagle,* the lunar landing vehicle. *Eagle*'s automatic pilot took over after the two craft separated, guiding it to a preprogrammed landing site, but as they neared the moon's surface, Armstrong saw that the chosen spot was in a crater full of boulders. Reacting quickly, he took over the controls. The lunar craft had a limited supply of fuel, barely more than was needed to get back to the command module. With only three seconds

"Houston, Tranquillity Base here. The *Eagle* has landed."

Neil Armstrong, July 20, 1969

Apollo 11's lunar module heads back from the moon's surface to dock with the command module (inset, above). Shortly after Neil Armstrong and Buzz Aldrin completed their historic moonwalk, a small bouquet of flowers appeared on John F. Kennedy's grave with a note reading: "Mr. President, the Eagle has landed."

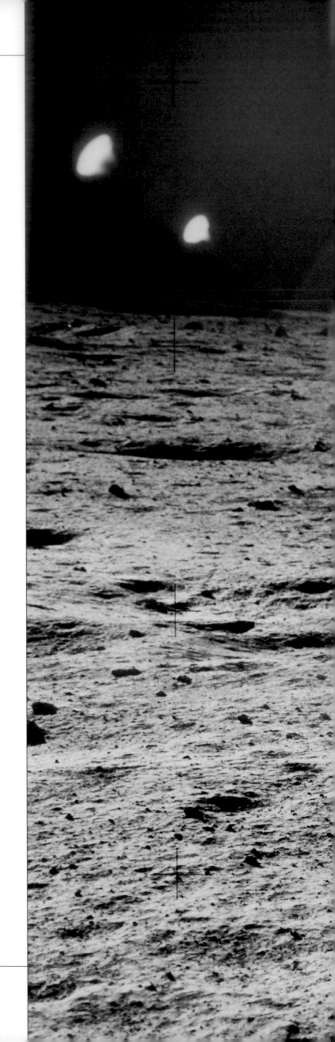

The second man to set foot on the moon, Buzz Aldrin stands in front of the lunar module, which Neil Armstrong—seen reflected in Aldrin's face shield—piloted. Armstrong landed the craft so gently that neither felt it touch down.

"Houston, we had a problem."

Jack Swigert, Apollo 13

As the crew of Apollo 13 struggles to stay alive, fellow astronauts (among them Alan Shepard, crouching in the foreground) and flight controllers hover anxiously over consoles in the Mission Operations Control Room in Houston. The Houston team and the crew devised a plan to use the moon-landing vehicle as a lifeboat after an explosion put the command module out of commission.

to spare, Armstrong put the *Eagle* down safely. And a few hours later he fulfilled Kennedy's promise, taking "one small step for man, one giant leap for mankind" onto the moon's powdery surface.

Apollo 11 clearly demonstrated American supremacy in space. For their part, the Soviets had matched successes with setbacks, including the 1967 death of cosmonaut Vladimir Komarov, whose Soyuz capsule slammed into the ground at 400 mph when its parachutes tangled. By 1969, when a Soviet lunar rocket exploded soon after liftoff, the race was, for all practical purposes, over.

The Most Successful Failure. America continued sending men to the moon to explore and conduct experiments. On April 14, 1970, Apollo 13—carrying Jim Lovell, Jack Swigert, and Fred Haise—was more than halfway there when an explosion in the service module section of the command module knocked out the main power supply. Priorities suddenly shifted: The crew's sole mission now was to figure out how to get home alive. Their only realistic choice was to use the undamaged lunar module as a sort of lifeboat, but it had been designed to carry only two crew members for two days; the trip home would take the three men four days. Amid intense discussions with Houston controllers, the team came up with a plan.

The astronauts climbed out of their crippled capsule into the landing module, then shut down every piece of equipment they didn't absolutely need—including the computer. As temperatures in the lunar module plummeted to barely above freezing and moisture coated the instrument panels, they adapted portions of the command module's life-support equipment to fit the landing craft, rigging the parts together with bits of cardboard, plastic, and duct tape. Cramped, cold, and scared, they waited out the four anxiety-filled days it took to get back. Approaching earth, they returned to the nearly frozen command capsule for reentry, jettisoned their lifeboat and the damaged service module, and buckled in. When the capsule finally splashed down, the whole nation breathed a sigh of relief. Though the mission was deemed a failure, NASA officials called it "the most successful failure in the annals of spaceflight." It had proved again that well-trained, resourceful pilots could handle just about anything.

Near the end of their ordeal, the Apollo 13 crew got this view of the extensive damage that was suffered by the service module when an oxygen cylinder exploded.

Haggard but relieved, Apollo 13 astronauts Fred Haise, Jim Lovell, and Jack Swigert (left to right) acknowledge the cheers upon their safe return to earth. Said Swigert afterward, "Our teamwork was fantastic. We were one body with three heads and six hands."

Columbia lifts off on April 12, 1981, inaugurating the space shuttle program. The large expendable liquid-fuel booster, painted white here, was left unpainted later to save money; the twin solid-rocket boosters were recovered after launch and reused.

"Your whole soul knows when the solids light."

Joe Allen,
space shuttle physicist-astronaut

Wings for Space

In 1922, only a few years before he launched the world's first liquid-fuel rocket, Robert Goddard *(page 163)* had written: "There can be no thought of finishing, for . . . no matter how much progress one makes there is always the thrill of just beginning." And so it seemed for America's adventures in space. After the staggering achievement of putting men on the moon, the nation's fascination with space travel had begun to wane somewhat, and the exorbitant expense of each mission was provoking increasing criticism. It was time for a fresh start. President Richard Nixon got things going by calling for an effort to "take the astronomical costs out of astronautics," and in 1973 NASA made the first steps in this direction by resurrecting an old idea abandoned nearly a decade earlier: the X-20 "Dyna-Soar" *(page 166)*.

The original Dyna-Soar had been intended to fly into and then fly back from space, ready to be used again. But now NASA engineers decided on a significant adaptation that combined the best of two worlds. Like existing spacecraft, their vehicle would be blasted into space, attached to mammoth booster rockets; true to the Dyna-Soar, though, it would be able to fly back into earth's atmosphere on wings and then could be launched and flown again and again. Its creators soon dubbed the new craft a "space shuttle," proposing that in the future similar vessels would take civilian passengers into space. Initially, however, its mission would be to ferry not passengers but payloads—including satellites and research instruments—which would be carried aloft in the shuttle's mammoth cargo bay.

To increase the whole design's cost-effectiveness, engineers made the shuttle's two solid-fuel booster rockets reusable as well. Jettisoned two minutes after liftoff and slowed by parachutes during a 30-mile descent, they would be recovered from the ocean and readied for another launch. The large liquid-fuel booster tank to which the shuttle orbiter was attached at launch would be the only part not recycled: Eight minutes into the flight, it too would be jettisoned but would burn up as it fell through the atmosphere.

On April 12, 1981, the first shuttle, *Columbia,* was launched, and as Goddard had asserted, the nation caught the thrill of a new beginning. During the next two decades four more shuttles—*Challenger, Atlantis, Discovery,* and *Endeavor*—would take to the skies, each flight bringing new insights into the rewards and hazards of space travel.

More than 100 miles above the earth, a shuttle glides
silently through space. The cargo bay, whose doors
remain open during orbit, can carry new satellites aloft
and return damaged ones for repairs.

Astronaut Dale Gardner becomes his own spacecraft as he maneuvers toward a damaged satellite by firing the nitrogen-powered rocket thrusters of his Manned Maneuvering Unit. The disk-shaped device he holds will help him grab the satellite and bring it back to the shuttle, whose robotic arm is visible at far right.

During *Columbia*'s third mission, for example, engineers learned a valuable lesson in the thermodynamics of space. Pilots Jack Lousma and Gordon Fullerton were testing the orbiter's heat shields by positioning it with its belly toward the sun. Before they realized what was happening, the intense solar heat warped the whole craft, and its opened payload doors jammed. Since the shuttle could not safely return to earth with the cargo bay open, the crew found themselves in a very perilous situation. Hoping to even out the thermal expansion and free the doors, they rolled the entire craft as if it were on a barbecue spit, exposing all sides to the sun. The strategy worked, and the doors closed.

Top-notch piloting skills proved invaluable during the shuttle *Challenger*'s fifth mission. One of the crew's tasks was to capture a damaged satellite that was spinning out of control. Using a new device called a Manned Maneuvering Unit (MMU) that allowed unfettered spacewalking, astronaut George Nelson left the *Challenger* and flew 50 yards through open space to catch the satellite and bring it back to the cargo bay. But when Nelson arrived at the satellite, he found that a solar blanket, which was not shown on the satellite's blueprints, covered the targeted grip; unable to grab on, he had to return to the shuttle empty-handed. In a last-ditch effort, Commander Robert Crippen, experienced in piloting high-performance military aircraft, brought the shuttle in close enough to the satellite— barely avoiding its extended solar arrays— for crew member Terry Hart to seize it with the shuttle's robotic arm.

Returning from its second mission after 54 hours in space, Columbia touches down on a runway at Edwards Air Force Base on November 14, 1981. A T-38 chase plane escorts the shuttle to the runway; its pilot assists with the landing by calling out Columbia's ever-decreasing speed and altitude.

"Zero g, and I feel fine."

John Glenn, 1962, 1998

John Glenn suits up again (opposite), this time for the shuttle Discovery mission in 1998. Thirty-six years after his historic Friendship 7 flight, the 77-year-old Glenn took part in a study on weightlessness, describing it in identical terms (quotation, above). His presence allowed the nation to recelebrate its achievements in space.

By 1986 the trusty *Challenger* had completed nine flights in its nearly three years of service, more than any of the others. On its tenth mission, however, the unthinkable occurred: Just 73 seconds after liftoff on January 28, 1986, with millions watching on television, the *Challenger* exploded and all seven crew members—including the first civilian astronaut, schoolteacher Christa McAuliffe—were killed. Investigators discovered that a defective joint in one of the solid-rocket boosters had triggered the explosion. The shuttle program was suspended for two years while new safety measures were created to prevent future tragedies.

Soon thereafter, the shuttles resumed their workhorse routine. But especially for those astronauts and researchers making their first trip, the flight would never be humdrum. Liftoff would always be the moment of highest drama, but the return from space could be equally compelling. The pilot commander begins the process by positioning the shuttle tail first and firing its maneuvering engines to slow it down, then repositions the craft nose first and belly down for reentry. The atmosphere itself slows the craft further as ceramic tiles on its underside glow bright orange from the heat of friction. After a series of S turns also designed to decrease its speed, the shuttle begins its final glide at 45,000 feet—still traveling at mach 3.5 and falling 10,000 feet per minute. With all fuel used up, the pilot must make a "dead stick" landing with no power and no second chance, approaching the runway at more than 200 miles per hour and at an angle six times as steep as that of a commercial jet. At 1,700 feet the pilot pulls the nose up, and at 90 feet the landing gear drops. Rear wheels touching first, the shuttle rolls to a stop, typically using nearly 10,000 feet of runway.

Although it now often flies missions with little or no fanfare, the shuttle was part of one more moment of glory as the century drew to a close. On October 29, 1998, John Glenn—now Senator Glenn—blasted into space for the second time, part of a seven-member crew on *Discovery.* For many who had seen him make history in *Friendship 7,* it was an occasion to remember how much had been achieved over the years. But it was also a chance to look back and realize that the story of flight, right back to its very beginning, had been a story with a human face.

ACKNOWLEDGMENTS

The editors wish to thank the following individuals and institutions for their valuable assistance in the preparation of this volume:

Guy Aceto, *Air Force* Magazine, Arlington, Va.; David Burgevin, Smithsonian Institution, Museum of American History, Washington, D.C.; Rep. Randy "Duke" Cunningham, Washington, D.C.; Anne De Atley, 11th Communications Squadron, Bolling Air Force Base, Washington, D.C.; M. E. Rhett Flater, American Helicopter Society, Alexandria, Va.; Mike Gentry, NASA/Media Services, Houston, Tex.; Cyndy Gilley, Do You Graphics, Woodbine, Md.; Barbara Hanson, United Air Lines Corporate Communications, Chicago; John Hill, Burlingame, Calif.; Mary Ison and Staff, Library of Congress, Washington, D.C.; Melissa Keiser, Smithsonian Institution, National Air and Space Museum, Washington, D.C.; Dana Kilanowski, Palmdale, Calif.; Sgt. Steve Leingang, Office of the Secretary of the the Air Force Public Affairs, Washington, D.C.; Eugene S. "Mac" McKendry, Cantil, Calif.; J. Campbell Martin, NASA Dryden Flight Research Center, Edwards Air Force Base, Calif.; Dave Menard, U.S. Air Force Museum, Wright Patterson Air Force Base, Ohio; Cliff Morris, Lancaster, Calif.; Dan O'Boyle, U.S. Army Public Affairs, Redstone Arsenal, Ala.; Dan Patterson, Dayton; Brent Perkins, Memphis Belle Association, Memphis; Bob Pepper, Public Affairs Office, Holloman Air Force Base, N.Mex.; Raymond L. Puffer, Air Force Flight Test Center/History Office, Edwards Air Force Base, Calif.; John Sanford, Wright State University, Dayton; Eric Schulzinger, Lockheed Martin Corp., Bethesda, Md.; Jeff Thurman, Johnson Controls, Inc., March ARB, Calif.; Kathy Vinson, Defense Visual Information Center-O-OPC, March ARB, Calif.; Brian York, Strategic Air Command Museum, Omaha.

Archives Neg. No. 428N-115-1725. **151**: U.S. Navy. **152, 153**: Video image courtesy CNN; Keith Chapman/Check Six, Tiburon, Calif. **154**: © Hans Halberstadt/Military Stock Photography, San Jose, Calif. **155**: CORBIS/Reuters. **156**: U.S. Air Force/DOD/March ARB, Calif. **157**: *Air Force* Magazine, Arlington, Va. **158, 159**: Randy G. Jolly/Arms Communications, Woodbridge, Va. **160, 161**: NASA; Frederick I. Ordway III Collection. **162**: CORBIS/Bettmann—NASM, Smithsonian Institution (SI Neg. No. 76-7559). **163**: NASM, Smithsonian Institution (SI Neg. No. A-45914-D)—NASA, courtesy NASM, Smithsonian Institution (SI Neg. No. A-48743-R)—Frederick I. Ordway III Collection—NASM, Smithsonian Institution (SI Neg. No. 77-15168). **164, 165**: AFFTC, History Office, Edwards AFB, Calif. **166**: NASM, Smithsonian Institution (SI Neg. No. 83-309). **167**: NASA—photo by Mark Avino, NASM, Smithsonian Institution (SI Neg. No. 95-8269). **168**: TASS/Sovfoto/Eastfoto, New York—Sovfoto/Eastfoto, New York. **169**: CORBIS/Bettmann. **170**: Ralph Morse, *Life* Magazine © Time Inc. **171**: NASA. **172**: Ralph Morse, *Life* Magazine © Time Inc.—CORBIS/Bettmann. **173**: Lynn Pelham/*Life* Magazine. **174, 175**: Astronaut Stafford/NASA; NASA. **176, 177**: NASA. **178, 179**: NASA; Neil A. Armstrong/NASA. **180-185**: NASA. **186**: Hank Morgan, Stamford, Conn. **187**: Ralph Morse.

BIBLIOGRAPHY

BOOKS

Aldrin, Buzz. *Men from Earth.* New York: Bantam Books, 1989.

Allen, Thomas B., F. Clifton Berry, and Norman Polmar. *CNN War in the Gulf.* Atlanta: Turner Publishing, 1991.

Almond, Peter. *Aviation: The Early Years.* London: Hulton Getty Picture Collection, 1997.

American Heritage History of Flight. New York: American Heritage, 1962.

Apollo Expedition to the Moon. Ed. by Edgar M. Cortright. Washington, D.C.: NASA, 1975.

Barlett, Donald L., and James B. Steele. *Empire: The Life, Legend, and Madness of Howard Hughes.* New York: Norton, 1979.

Berg, A. Scott. *Lindbergh.* New York: G. P. Putnam, 1998.

Bond, Peter. *Reaching for the Stars: The Illustrated History of Manned Spaceflight.* London: Cassell, 1993.

Booth, Nicholas. *Space: The Next 100 Years.* New York: Orion Books, 1990.

Boyne, Walter J. *The Smithsonian Book of Flight.* Washington, D.C.: Smithsonian Books, 1987.

Brennan, Dennis. *Adventures in Courage: The Skymasters.* Chicago: Reilly & Lee, 1968.

Brown, Peter Harry, and Pat H. Broeske. *Howard Hughes: The Untold Story.* New York: Dutton, 1996.

Burrows, William E. *This New Ocean: The Story of the First Space Age.* New York: Random House, 1998.

Butler, Susan. *East to the Dawn: The Life of Amelia Earhart.* Reading, Mass.: Addison-Wesley, 1997.

Chaikin, Andrew. *Air and Space: The National Air and Space Museum Story of Flight.* Boston: Bulfinch Press, 1997.

Costello, John, and Terry Hughes. *The Concorde Conspiracy.* New York: Charles Scribner's Sons, 1976.

Crouch, Tom D. *The Bishop's Boys: A Life of Wilbur and Orville Wright.* New York: W. W. Norton, 1989.

Cunningham, Randy. *Fox Two.* Mesa, Ariz.: Champlin Fighter Museum, 1984.

Dorr, Robert F. *Air War Hanoi.* New York: Blandford Press, 1988.

Duerksen, Menno. *The Memphis Belle.* Memphis: Memphis Belle Memorial Association, 1987.

Earhart, Amelia. *Last Flight.* New York: Orion Books, 1937.

The Epic of Flight (23 vols.). Alexandria, Va., Time-Life Books, 1980-1983.

Ethell, Jeffrey L. *Frontiers of Flight.* Washington, D.C.: Smithsonian Books, 1992.

Ethell, Jeffrey, and Alfred Price. *One Day in a Long War: May 10, 1972, Air War, North Vietnam.* New York: Random House, 1989.

Foxworth, Thomas G. *The Speed Seekers.* New York: Doubleday, [1976].

Genat, Robert. *Choppers: Thunder in the Sky.* New York: MetroBooks, 1998.

Glines, Carroll V. *Jimmy Doolittle: Daredevil Aviator and Scientist.* New York: Macmillan, 1972.

Glines, Carroll V., and Wendell F. Moseley. *The Story of a Fabulous Airplane: The DC-3.* Philadelphia: J. B. Lippincott, 1966.

Guilmartin, John, Jr., and Michael O'Leary. *Helicopters.* New York: Bantam Books, 1988.

Harrison, James P. *Mastering the Sky.* New York: Sarpedon, 1996.

Hook, Jason. *Twenty Names in Aviation.* New York: Marshall Cavendish, 1990.

Hoyt, Edwin P. *The Airmen.* New York: McGraw-Hill, 1990.

Johnston, A. M. *Tex Johnston: Jet-Age Test Pilot.* Washington, D.C.: Smithsonian Institution Press, 1991.

Kilduff, Peter. *Richthofen: Beyond the Legend of the Red Baron.* New York: John Wiley & Sons, 1993.

Lindbergh, Charles A. *The Spirit of St. Louis.* New York: Charles Scribner's Sons, 1953.

Lopez, Donald S. *Aviation: A Smithsonian Guide.* New York: Macmillan, 1995.

Macmillan, Norman. *Great Airmen.* New York: St. Martin's Press, 1957.

Morrocco, John. *Rain of Fire: Air War, 1969-1973* (The Vietnam Experience series). Boston: Boston Publishing, 1985.

Morrow, John H., Jr. *The Great War in the Air: Military Aviation from 1909-1921.* Washington, D.C.: Smithsonian Institution Press, 1993.

Murphy, Edward F. *Heroes of World War II.* Novato, Calif.: Presidio, 1990.

The New Face of War (9 vols.). Alexandria, Va.: Time-Life Books, 1990-1992.

Nowarra, H. J., and Kimbrough S. Brown, comps. *Von Richthofen and the Flying Circus.* Ed by Bruce Robertson. Letchworth, Herts, England: Harleyford, 1964.

Patterson, Dan. *American Eagles: A History of the United States Air Force.* Charlottesville, Va.: Howell Press, 1997.

Rabinowitz, Harold. *Conquer the Sky: Great Moments in Aviation.* New York: MetroBooks, 1996.

Rich, Ben R., and Leo Janos. *Skunk Works: A Personal Memoir of My Years at Lockheed.* Boston: Little, Brown, 1994.

Rickenbacker, Edward V. *Fighting the Flying Circus.* New York: Frederick A. Stokes, 1919.

Roseberry, C. R.:
 The Challenging Skies: The Colorful Story of Aviation's Most Exciting Years, 1919-1939. Garden City, N.Y.: Doubleday, 1966.
 Glenn Curtiss: Pioneer of Flight. Syracuse, N.Y.: Syracuse University Press, 1991.

Scharff, Robert, and Walter S. Taylor. *Over Land and Sea: A Biography of Glenn Hammond Curtiss.* New York: David McKay, 1968.

Spick, Mike. *Milestones of Manned Flight.* New York: Smithmark, 1994.

Stuhlinger, Ernst, and Frederick I. Ordway III. *Wernher von Braun: Crusader for Space.* Malabar, Fla.: Krieger, 1994.

Sunderman, James F., ed. *Early Air Pioneers: 1862-1935.* New York: Franklin Watts, 1961.

Taylor, Richard. *The First Solo Flight around the World: The Story of Wiley Post and His Airplane the Winnie Mae.* New York: Franklin Watts, 1993.

Tessendorf, K. C. *Barnstormers & Daredevils.* New York: Atheneum, 1988.

Thompson, Milton O. *At the Edge of Space: The X-15 Flight Program.* Washington, D.C.: Smithsonian Institution Press, 1992.

The Vietnam War: The Illustrated History of the Conflict in Southeast Asia. New York: Crown, 1983.

Von Braun, Wernher, and Frederick I. Ordway III. *History of Rocketry & Space Travel.* New York: Thomas Y. Crowell, 1975.

World War II (39 vols.). Alexandria, Va., Time-Life Books, 1976-1983.

Yeager, Chuck, et al. *The Quest for Mach One: A First-Person Account of Breaking the Sound Barrier.* New York: Penguin Studio, 1997.

Yeager, Chuck, and Leo Janos. *Yeager: An Autobiography.* Toronto: Bantam Books, 1985.

Yenne, Bill. *Legends of Flight.* Lincolnwood, Ill.: Publications International, 1997.

Zisfein, Melvin B. *Flight: A Panorama of Aviation.* New York: Pantheon Books, 1981.

PERIODICALS

Burrows, Larry. "One Ride with Yankee." *Life,* April 16, 1965.
Canan, James W. "Lesson Number One." *Air Force,* October 1991.
Dille, John. "Good Copters, but Bum Tactics." *Life,* April 16, 1965.
Karten, Dave. "SAC." *The Airman,* February 1958.
"Khrushchev's Pre-Summit Spy Cry." *Life,* May 16, 1960.
Mackenzie, Richard. "Apache Attack." *Air Force,* October 1991.
McMichael, William H. "First Shots Fired in Anger." *Soldiers,* April 1991.

Magnuson, Ed. "Brace! Brace! Brace!" *Time,* July 31, 1989.
Stanglin, Douglas, Susan Headden, and Peter Cary. "Secrets of the Cold War." *U.S. News & World Report,* March 15, 1993.
Stanglin, Douglas, and Sergei Kuznetsov. "A New Look at the U-2 Case." *U.S. News & World Report,* March 15, 1993.
Thomas, Evan, and John Barry. "War's New Science." *Newsweek,* February 18, 1991.
Thompson, Mark. "How We Fight." *Time,* April 26, 1999.

INDEX

Numerals in italics indicate an illustration of the subject mentioned.

Time-Life Books is a division of Time Life Inc.

TIME LIFE INC.
PRESIDENT and CEO: George Artandi

TIME-LIFE BOOKS
PUBLISHER/MANAGING EDITOR: Neil Kagan
VICE PRESIDENT, MARKETING: Joseph A. Kuna
VICE PRESIDENT, NEW PRODUCT DEVELOPMENT:
Amy Golden

OUR AMERICAN CENTURY

EDITORS: Loretta Britten, Paul Mathless
DIRECTOR, NEW PRODUCT DEVELOPMENT:
Elizabeth D. Ward
DIRECTOR OF MARKETING: Pamela R. Farrell

Century of Flight
Editor: Robert Somerville
Deputy Editor: Mary Mayberry
Design Director: Tina Taylor
Associate Editor/Research and Writing: Annette Scarpitta
Associate Marketing Manager: Teri Miller
Picture Associate: Anne Whittle
Technical Art Specialist: John Drummond
Senior Copyeditors: Anne Farr, Judith Klein
Photo Coordinator: Betty H. Weatherley
Editorial Assistant: Christine Higgins

Design for **Our American Century** by Antonio Alcalá,
Studio A, Alexandria, Virginia.

Special Contributors: Karen Sweet (editing); Ronald H. Bailey,
Constance Buchanan, Leo Janos (writing); Stephanie Henke,
James Michael Lynch, Marilyn Terrell (research-writing);
Constance Contreras, Christine Hauser, Daniel Kulpinski, Jane
Martin, Elizabeth Thompson (research); Richard Friend (design);
Susan Nedrow (index).

Correspondents: Maria Vincenza Aloisi (Paris), Christine Hinze
(London), Christina Lieberman (New York).
Valuable assistance was also provided by: Angelika Lemmer
(Bonn), Midori Kai, Tamae Yoshida (Tokyo).

Director of Finance: Christopher Hearing
Directors of Book Production: Marjann Caldwell, Patricia Pascale
Director of Publishing Technology: Betsi McGrath
Director of Photography and Research: John Conrad Weiser
Director of Editorial Administration: Barbara Levitt
Manager, Technical Services: Anne Topp
Senior Production Manager: Ken Sabol
Production Manager: Virginia Reardon
Quality Assurance Manager: James King
Chief Librarian: Louise D. Forstall

Separations by the Time-Life Imaging Department

EDITORIAL CONSULTANT
Richard B. Stolley is currently senior editorial adviser at Time
Inc. After 19 years at *Life* magazine as a reporter, bureau chief,
and assistant managing editor, he became the first managing
editor of *People* magazine, a position he held with great success
for eight years. He then returned to *Life* magazine as managing
editor and later served as editorial director for all Time Inc.
magazines. In 1997 Stolley received the Henry Johnson Fisher
Award for Lifetime Achievement, the magazine industry's
highest honor.

Library of Congress Cataloging-in Publication Data
Century of flight / by the editors of Time-Life Books.
p. cm.—(Our American century)
Includes bibliographical references and index.
ISBN 0-7835-5514-8
1. Aeronautics—History.   I. Time-Life Books.   II. Series.
TL515.C36   1999
629.13'09—dc21   99-29398
                                                               CIP

Other History Publications:

On the cover:
*Airplane pilot and international playboy Hubert Latham soars in
solitary splendor above the French coastline in his elegant Antoinette
monoplane in the summer of 1909, days before he failed in an attempt to cross the English Channel. Courageous and cool under pressure, Latham epitomized the dashing pilots of the day—anxious to
break new ground while they pushed their delicate machines to fly
higher and faster and farther. Faces representing a century of flight
are featured across the top of the cover: General Billy Mitchell, ad-
venturer Amelia Earhart, millionaire industrialist Howard Hughes,
air force test pilot Chuck Yeager, head of the Strategic Air Command
General Curtis LeMay, and a fighter pilot in the cockpit of his F-16.*